BMW 6-SERIES

BMW 6-SERIES

Jeremy Walton

ARCO PUBLISHING, INC.
NEW YORK

First published 1985
© Jeremy Walton
ISBN 0-668-06147-2

Library of Congress Catalog Card Number 84-70869

ISBN 0 947784 016

Published in the USA by Arco Publishing Inc
215 Park Avenue South, New York, N.Y. 10003

Filmset by Grange Filmsetting Limited, Birmingham
Printed and bound in Great Britain
by Biddles of Guildford.

Acknowledgements

I think Julian Watson at Cadogan Books deserves 'pole position' in this section, as I most certainly would not have written anything on this subject without his persistence and good-humoured persuasion . . .

Naturally my primary editorial thanks are to BMW in Munich and Great Britain. As ever Michael Schimpke ensured that I had access to the men and machinery, but we would have not had such a wealth of material without Peter Zollner's Achiv paradise, 'Claudi's' coffee and Uwe Mahla's BMW Motorsport guidance. My thanks to all those, who are named in the relevant chapters, for the interviews they gave. Also in Bavaria I must repeat a debt of editorial and personal thanks to Alpina's Burkard Bovensiepen, who tutored me through BMW's sporting achievements originally and continues to provide not only first class motor cars, but hospitality that improves each time I return. Visiting Burkard's cellars would be reason enough for my continuing BMW enthusiasm . . .

In Britain Raymond Playfoot has once again put up with my unreasonable demands with his now legendary speed and efficiency. His assistants always seem to graduate from some special Raymond charm school, and Michele Cory maintains the standard. The only thing I cannot forgive is that the 6-Series used to complete this book's Munich research was sold to another journalist before I could get a second mortgage on a home that was for sale anyway . . !

I did not interview Dieter Stappert, BMW Competitions Director for this title specifically, but his informative leadership and often telephonic company maintains my BMW interest. Much of the detail 635 racing knowledge I owe to Malcolm Gartlan and Ted Grace, the men behind Frank Sytner's British BMW, who took me to Munich when they negotiated the purchase of their first 635 racer. I have known both before and since their BMW CSL-Alpina days, when Brian Muir and Niki Lauda graced the cockpit of their winning BMW over a decade ago. They have unfailingly treated me fairly and added to a store of racing lore in each conversation.

Of the racing drivers mentioned Hans Joachim 'Striezel' Stuck, Dieter Quester and Tom Walkinshaw have always been helpful, even when talking to journalists was priority 410 on their minds . . .

Photographically I took more pictures than usual but remain indebted to BMW themselves (particularly Munich's resources), London Art Tech at Standard House, and the talented artists who do so much to make BMW understandable in their fabulous cutaways.

Personally I can only say that my wife Patricia withstood my assaults on the English language again with a course on the use of begin, begun and began and regular spelling bees. I was accompanied on the Munich Foray by Peter Newton, editor of Cars & Car Conversions in Croydon. I would not have attempted the rigorous interview and research schedule without his invaluable company. I must apologise to Fiona, for taking her new husband away and forcing him to drink the alcoholic substances he so disdains, but hope she agrees it was all in a Good Cause.

JEREMY WALTON

Middle Assendon

July 1984

CONTENTS

Chapter One

BMW: Born, Reborn and Born Again

From the sleek shine of 6-Series BMW coupé craftsmanship back to the origins of Bayerischen Motoren Werke, which supplied those now prestigious BMW initials, is a long and convoluted story. For BMW sprang from a dozen different origins, even prior to the first use of those initials to designate a new force in aero engine manufacture from March 7th 1916. The researcher is faced with myriad deals, financial crises and two World Wars that directly affected BMW fortunes. Leaving one in a state of some admiration for the company's survival, never mind its present awesome prosperity as the manufacturer of 421,000 vehicles a year (1983's record), and equally impressive profits of the kind that have created that inspired four cylinder HQ building opposite Munich's *Olympiapark*.

Can this eighties BMW, planning a *third* Bavarian factory to ease the bulging seams of Munich–Milbertshofen (the original airfield and aero-engine works area of the World War I era) and a Dingolfing plant, created out of the absorption of Glas in the sixties; can this *really* be the same company as had to make saucepans from aluminium scraps, after facing the full fury of the Allied air assaults in the forties?

Surely this epitome of the West German post-war revival could not have been facing life as a Mercedes division as recently as 1959? Then BMW had reeled onto the ringside ropes of motor manufacturing, with a model mix that plunged from low volume V8s to Isetta-BMW bubble cars. Can it also be true that these providers of the supremely logical 3, 5, 6, and 7-Series have any affiliation with East Germany's current home for Wartburg at Eisenach? Or that BMW started car manufacture with a licence to pump out British Austin Sevens?

All these queries are actually factual statements of BMW's tortuous

1

Aero engines were the original reason for a Bavarian Motor Works, and their radial designs (such as this 10-cylinder) were particularly effective. The company was not left behind in the adoption of the jet aero engine either, claiming 'the world's first series production jet engine to power an aircraft', for the 109-003 that BMW's 47,000 plus workforce of 1943 manufactured.

history, but a few general recollections make such a twisted tale easily understood. Whether manufacturing aero engines for, and between two World Wars. Or producing the kind of cars and motorcycles that attract such fierce customer loyalty that the legend-spinner's task is made redundant, BMW's title is absolutely apt: Bavarian *Motor* Works make superb *engines* that really have made a mark on land, sea and air history.

Look back through the company records and the constant competitive element is always present, whether in outright wartime conditions, or in today's popular image as the 600-800bhp turbo powerhouse behind 1983 Parmalat-Brabham World Champion, Nelson Piquet. They really are supreme competitors down in Bavaria . . .

The subject of this book, the two door 6-Series coupé, illustrates BMW tradition well. Originally it was conceived as an elegant upmarket move from the popular sporting coupés of 1968-75, a series of Karmann-bodied two doors that had set the racing world on its ear with the use of a 'Batmobile' wing set for CSL competition models that eventually ended up bearing mighty Munich 24-valve motors of 470 horsepower. BMW decided that a touch more civilisation was needed in the 6-Series successor and, using the 5-Series saloon as a literal base, they created a line of luxury coupés, then culminating in the 3.3 litre fuel injection 633 CSi (a model that lived in the America of the eighties with a full set of emission controls shared with the large 7-Series saloon, 733i).

However, within a couple of years BMW were forced to return to their sporting heritage with the 635 CSi, a 135mph plus derivative that used the cylinder block of the previously 'racing-only' $3\frac{1}{2}$ litre size created by BMW Motorsport engine supremo Paul Rosche's versatile staff. It was not long before the 635 was notching up European saloon car championship titles with the same abandon as the earlier coupés.

Finally the 6-Series returned even more powerfully to earlier BMW racing success, a 286bhp version of the 24-valve engine being installed in the M for Motorsport 635 that provided BMW with a 150mph M635 CSi coupé to prowl Porsche-infested Autobahns with pride! As we shall see that remarkable 4 valve per cylinder six had gone through many development stages between upholding racing honour in the coupé and providing growling supercar performance in the mid-engine M1 of 1979-80. Throughout the story the respect BMW have earned as providers of power plants in traditionally conscientiously crafted automobiles is apparent.

There have been mistakes of course, some of them in far more public arenas than sniping rivals like to occupy, but when you look over the solid worth of the subtle 6-Series, it is obvious that BMW created a coupé worthy of their fascinating heritage . . .

Roots

Tracing the origins of BMW in car manufacture means travelling to the East German town of Eisenach and remembering December 3rd 1896. It was here in the Thuringia's forested and hilly terrain that armaments

Established before the turn of the century as a manufacturing base, Eisenach is now within the borders of East Germany. BMW took over the Dixi works in October 1928, but BMW badges did not dominate the Austin 7-based cars they made, until 1929.

specialist and multi-talented inventor Dr Heinrich Ehrhardt formed Fahrzeugfabrik Eisenach on that date. Dr Ehrhardt had already played a prominent role in the emergence of Rhinemetall Konzern, second only to Krupp in the scale of armaments manufacture within Germany.

In view of their connections it was not surprising that the first Eisenach vehicles were military designs such as munitions carriers, ambulances and gun carriages, but that was not an overwhelming commercial success. Thus in 1898 Ehrhardt foresaw modern industry practice and made an agreement with Decauville in France to make a small, voiturette, class of car. By the turn of the century they were using the emblem and name of the Wartburg castle that overlooks Eisenach. Even in 1899 BMW's Wartburg forbears were racing up to then dizzy heights of 37mph – it sounds better as the original 60km/h! – and winning attention at the Berlin motor show of the period. They even got around to exporting a machine known as the Cosmobile to the USA.

From 1889 to 1903 it is estimated that about 250 Wartburg cars were delivered from Eisenach, many under the Decauville agreement, but Wartburgs also came in fierce racing guises. In 1902 they had a four cylinder delivering about 22bhp from 3.1 litres and the sophistication of a five speed gearbox to enable them to reach slightly beyond Britain's 70mph limit of 82 years later!

Ehrhardt resigned the chair at Eisenach to form his own company away from Rhinemetall, who also got rid of the embryo Wartburg outfit, Ehrhardt leaving in 1903. The first use of the Dixi name had occurred some time before the 1904 Frankfurt Motor Show (today the biggest motor show in Europe), but it was confirmed with a touring car displayed under that name for this important hardy annual.

Dixi evolved from 1904 to 1927, manufacturing giant 7.3 litre racing and touring cars *en route*, along with lorries that naturally found increased demand through the First World War. After hostilities concluded Eisenach's Dixi marque were in trouble, along with much of the rest of German industry and the take-over trail that leads to BMW today began. First Gothaer Wagonfabrik took on the Eisenach manufacturers, but they were in no fit state to resist the advances of a well known contemporary financier, Jacob Schapiro. Look through the histories of NSU and Mercedes/Daimler-Benz and you will find he was involved with them, as well as other now defunct marques such as

Cyklon and Hansa. Altogether 15,822 vehicles were reckoned to have been made at Eisenach before BMW stepped in on October 1st 1928. Now, let us look back to see where the men of Munich generated enough impetus in inflation-stricken twenties Germany to afford a debt-ridden Dixi empire . . .

Again military contracts feature in such history, together with two Austrians and a German from the Swabian district that encompasses the home of Mercedes and Porsche in Stuttgart. Austrian engineering graduate Franz Joseph Popp was sent to study aero engineering manufacturing techniques at Daimler and Benz in 1914 with a view to making such motors at the works of his employers, AEG-Union in Vienna. The plan did not reach fruition, but Popp learned enough to want to be further involved. Ironically the change came in the form of a marine authority engine contract for aero engines awarded to Rapp motor works in Munich, which Popp was asked to oversee.

The young (he was under twenty at the outbreak of war) Popp did not like what he saw in terms of the incompetence displayed by Rapp's production methods. Popp enlisted the help of a man who really can take the credit for much of BMW's early engines engineering reputation: Dr Max Friz. Popp and Friz were bankrolled by Camillo Castiglioni and were all set for a career in the provision of wartime aeronautical engines; Friz a former Daimler designer, who had brought with him the concept of a high performance aero engine, after a pay dispute with his former employers at Daimler.

For the purist it should be noted that there were two 1916 dates that featured formation of companies entitled to use BMW initials: July 20th 1916 saw the creation of Bayerische Motorenwerke GmbH from the unified Gustav Rau and Rapp Motorenwerke. Yet today's company name, proudly displayed over the portals of the four cylinder building, Bayerischen Motoren Werke AG, came when Castiglioni purchased the Lerchenauer Strasse site next to the post-war defunct Bavarian Aeroplane Works. They had registered the name that is used today in the Munich city register on that March 7th 1916 date we gave earlier. Confused? There's more to come . . .

The end of the war saw BMW with less than 100 of the planned 2000 Friz-designed BMW 111a aero motors delivered, and a ban on further German manufacture of such power plants.

Another consistently successful competition activity was that on two wheels, although the three wheeler sidecars went on winning with the twenties-designed Boxer (opposed cylinders) engine that can be so clearly seen in this fine action picture, long after the Japanese invasion of solo motorcycle racing.

7

They got by with various static motors and the fabrication of brake systems for the railway system, but the BMW of today became recognisable when the Friz flat twin motorcycle motor joined the R32 double tube frame bike, along with shaft drive. Principles that live on in the eighties, although it is worth noting that BMW motorcycles are not manufactured in Munich, but in Berlin, a remark that applies with equal force to the new four cylinder K-series, as well as the flat twin descendants of the Friz era, which commenced production in 1923.

BMW were back in the aero business for engine manufacture by 1924, but chief engineer and co-founder Franz Popp wanted a further diversification into the small car business. BMW looked at a number of existing options, including a front drive machine, boxer, opposed cylinder, principles shared with BMW motorcycle philosophy as an obvious attraction.

When BMW opted out of this SHW prototype series there was an opportunity to acquire Dixi at Eisenach. Like most others in the Germany of the twenties, BMW were pretty near broke in the conventional banking sense. Financial magician Camillo Castiglioni performed with his customary persuasive manner and the share capital was upped some 60 per cent to allow BMW financial control at Eisenach during November 1928, although the deal was actually recognised when Dixi at Eisenach became a BMW subsidiary from October 1st that year.

With the 1200 Dixi employees came a ready-made production car that BMW decided to keep on, and which eventually became the first BMW four wheeler. The machine was known as the Dixi 3/15, but it was actually a modified Austin Seven that the wheeling and dealing Mr Schapiro had acquired for Dixi, when it was realised they could no longer afford to develop their own machinery.

The first 100 Austin Sevens came direct from the UK and were on sale by April 1927, complete with RHD! However when producing commenced in Germany LHD was installed, along with sophistications such as battery ignition. Some such cars were made late in 1927 and were sold from the opening month of 1928. When BMW took over they left the Dixi badge and the car alone until July 1929, when the BMW badge and a series of changes showed that the new masters were restless to exploit their own engineering ideas for light cars.

Gradually modifying the Seven concept further and further–includ-

September 5th 1931, less than three years since BMW took over Dixi's factories and debts (rather more than anticipated!) and the 25,000th BMW 3/15 adaptation of the Austin Seven four cylinder saloon has left the Eisenach works. Only another 365 were made before production of the British licensed Seven stopped in March 1932.

9

The 1933-36 BMW 303 introduced two significant BMW traditions, that for inline six cylinder engines and the Nierenformig, *or kidney-shaped, front grille. Then of 1173cc and 30bhp, this six cylinder breed provided the basis for the 1.9 litre and 2-litre BMW sixes that were so widely copied in countries outside West Germany during the post war years. In the 303 the 1.2 litre provides about 60mph and an overall 28mpg.*

ing a batch of derivatives for army use and an apparently rather unpleasant swing *front* axle–BMW tramped their way inexorably toward a true BMW car; by 1932 they had delivered over 25,000 Seven 'cousins' but in March they ceased to be licencees of the British small car.

That spring BMW brought their own 3/20 to the market place, which still had a small (782cc) four cylinder producing 20bhp at 3500rpm with Overhead Valves (OHV), rather than the Seven's sidevalve engine, which was providing 15 horsepower at 3000rpm on the same 5.6:1 compression ratio. Aah, those were the low-stressed days . . .

The first BMW had a three speed gearbox and would reach around 50mph, with BMW recalling a 37mpg equivalent as typical of its everyday consumption. It weighed a lot more than the earlier Seven-derived cars, its body built by Daimler-Benz at Sindelfingen: if memory serves, that is the site Mercedes now use to build the deadly rival to BMW's 3-series, the 190! In those pre-World War II days Stuttgart, Munich and Eisenach were on exceptionally friendly terms, there being plenty of aero-engine work for everyone as the emphasis returned to military manufacturing.

In fact you could see that BMW had returned to their original first love of performance aero engines by analysing the 1933 deployment of staff: over half were working on the revived aero industry's behalf . . . As the second bout of World War approached, BMW diversified their activities beyond engine manufacture, but the car business was far from neglected.

Increasing general company prosperity allowed funds for further BMW model development. The six cylinder inline engine design that would lead to the now highly-prized 328 classic sports car traced its roots back to the 1933 BMW 303. This was a modest looking saloon, but it ran smoothly and sweetly to its 56mph maximum. This BMW engine had 30bhp delivered from the usual long stroke relative to bore ratio of the period (56×80mm gave 1173cc).

The sixes continued with the 1934-37 BMW 315 of 1490cc and 34 horsepower, which had a sporting 315/1 brother that had the same cubic capacity, but featuring *three* sidedraught Solex carburettors and a 6.8:1 compression ratio, instead of the traditional ex-Seven 5.6:1cr. This brought 40bhp at 4300rpm, and a capacity for tackling then newish autobahnen at up to 75mph. Snigger if you like, but with a 55mph limit currently enforced in the USA, 70mph in Britain, and limits on all but the autobahns of 1984 Germany, envy might be a more relevant emotion to feel for the 230 or so lucky 315/1 owners of 1934-37 in their rakish two seaters.

The BMW sporting tradition on four wheels can be traced back to rakish machines such as this 315/1 Sport of 1934-36. It used a 1911cc version of the pre-war BMW six, it was fed by triple Solex carburettors and could reach 75mph in normal road trim.

11

Most famous pre-war BMW of all, and the ultimate expression of their six cylinder sporting philosophy at the time, was the 328. Some 462 of these 1936-39 machines were made, many racing at much higher speeds than the 93mph the roadgoing model could achieve from 1971cc punching out 80bhp. It was this 2-litre unit that was to stay in production for so many varied factories and duties during postwar years.

There were plenty of other six cylinder alternatives produced in comparatively small numbers by BMW at the Eisenach of the 1930s: 319/1 with 55bhp from the 1911cc engine it shared with the less exotically carburated 319 and 329. Yet, most interest was generated, and continues to be generated if you are lucky enough to hear one operate with sewing machine precision and racing-orientated exhaust, by BMW's 328. Announced by the simple expedient of having Ernst Henne pound around the Nurburgring to victory in the Eifelrennen of June 1936, the 328 was sold from February 1937 with either Hurth or ZF four speed gearboxes and a production engine capacity of 1971cc extracted from a bore and stroke of 66×96mm. This was the faithful OHV BMW inline six. Complete with a then high 7.6:1 compression ratio and three Solex 30mm downdraught carburettors, it punched out 80bhp at a then comparatively high 5000rpm.

That power output was enough to realise over 93mph with likely near-20mpg fuel consumption. However most of the 462 BMW 328s produced probably had modifications of some sort applied, if not during the thirties, then almost certainly during or after that War, when a lot of 328 technology re-emerged in various guises as enthusiasts endeavoured to enjoy motor sport/found a new sports marque. For BMW, getting back on their feet post-World War II would probably be the hardest task ever faced by this resourceful concern. The works at Milbertshofen had naturally been a number 1 allied target for saturation bombing

Blasted from the air, 24 hours a day. Munich 1945, the unlikely site for a new BMW car manufacturing base, but not until the 1950s.

13

techniques whilst Eisenach, although it is geographically to the west of Munich, fell into the arms of the eastern-based Soviet Army. Even in 1945 Eisenach had started to produce saloons based around the rugged 1971cc six under the Soviet-controlled brand name Autovelo BMW 321.

It took BMW, now regrouped solely in Munich after the loss of Eisenach and Brandenburg (Berlin) until 1947 to resume motorcycle manufacture (R 24). Prior to which date they had survived with making the cooking utensils referred to earlier, although even that was a major achievement because US-occupied Munich had originally received instructions that BMW was to be subject to complete confiscation of all assets.

Even without that drastic measure BMW could only sit on the sidelines in the immediate post-war years whilst concerns such as the Bristol Aircraft Co in Britain were awarded 'the spoils of war' in the form of the inline six cylinder car engine, which they developed to consistently high power outputs (105bhp in the 405) and finally stretched to 2.2 litres in the 406, which did not cease production until 1961. So the design had basically been on the motoring scene in four very different decades! Incidentally the link between Bristol and BMW was via AFN's H. J. Aldington, a director of Bristol and responsible for AFN's thirties introduction of BMW to the British market: indeed AFN made various 328-derived sports cars until the late fifties, but are today much better known through their association with Porsche GB.

BMW also had to exhume the 1971cc inline six cylinder engine for their first post-war model, the 501 saloon. This rotund machine with its unique bevel gear steering system, and a gearbox mounted virtually under the front seats, connected forward by a stubby propshaft, was shown at the Frankfurt salon of 1951, even though BMW had no tools to press-stamp its body! They managed to make the first 501s on their stout tubular chassis during 1952, using the facilities of Bauer at Stuttgart—who eventually contributed much to mid-engined M1 construction in 1979-80 as well. BMW's own press steel works were not available until 1955.

These 65 horsepower 501 saloons could waddle up to 84mph despite their 1340kg/2948lb girth, but it understandably took them about 27 seconds to reach 100kph (62mph) from rest; acceleration not even up to pre-war levels. Germany's post-war production V8, constructed in aluminium alloy, solved the 501's pace problems from 1954 onward with an initial 90bhp that had reached 160bhp in the 1962-65 ancestors of today's BMW coupés: BMW's elegant 3200 CS.

The 90° V8 engine started life with a capacity of 2580cc, featuring virtually square dimensions of 74×75mm, but measured 3168cc (82×75mm) by the 1956-59 production span of the rare but extremely stylish 503 and 507. Both were styled by Graf Goertz and were based on the 501/502 saloon running gear, establishing a post-war BMW tradition for sporting cousins to production saloons that was later transferred to the coupé category.

Although the 252 BMW 507s constructed were capable of stomping to 137 mph and 0-63mph in 11.5 seconds, nearly thirty years ago, the low production runs of these and other large BMWs were obviously not

The BMW 501 and 502 series of large saloons attracted publicity and respect, typified by this picture of the TV police car in the series Hier Isar 12 . . *of the fifties. Income from these large cars, and minuscule machinery like the BMW Isetta three and four wheeler 'bubble cars' was insufficient. The 1954 alloy V8 for the 502 was Germany's first eight cylinder in production postwar, and it developed into the 3.2 litre capable of producing 140 horsepower and 110mph in this 4000lb plus limousine. Some pursuit car . . .!*

Coupé version of the BMW 700 with its motorcycle-derived flat twin engine was a strong seller and a good motorsport class competitor, but still the company looked for middleweight salvation, and the money to produce such a car.

going to extract Munich from increasing financial woes. Motorcycles simply couldn't offset mounting losses in the car division, which offered big cars at one end of the scale (501, 502, 503 and 507) and flyweights like the 1955-62 Isetta 250 or the 1956-62 Isetta 300 with three and four wheel layout. There was simply nothing to offer the vital middle classes who had emerged into the boom class of revitalised Germany. The 600 four wheeler was a pace in the right direction, but it still had the flat twin motorcycle engine that also characterised the later, more successful 700s. Cash was needed to develop that middleweight contender and to progress the logical 700 development of 600 to 'hold the fort' until a $1\frac{1}{2}$ litre engined BMW could be introduced . . .

Losses were apparent in 1958 and by 1959 crisis point was reached. In December 1959 the Deutsche Bank even proposed a redevelopment and salvation plan that amounted to amalgamation with Mercedes-Benz. The shareholders, and particularly the BMW dealers, revolted at this strong medicine and banded together to fight with astonishing effect, under the leadership of Frankfurt lawyer Dr Friedrich Mathern. Aided by some capital from near-by MAN, the truck concern, the shareholders kept fighting until the Deutsche Bank and Mercedes effectively withdrew, Dr Mathern serving on the BMW board until 1966. Influencing BMW fortunes right into the eighties were the Quandt brothers, Herbert and Harald, who emerged as substantial stockholders during this period. Dr Herbert Quandt took the more personal interest in BMW and built on a 15 per cent shareholding to the point where he held voting control of more than half the shareholding capital!

A general meeting in November 1960 saw BMW pointed along its present success route, initially guided by Dr Johannes Semler. He had the confidence of increased capital and an extremely warm reception for the rear engine 700, which had debuted in 1959 and went on to sell over 181,000 derivatives in saloon and successful sporting coupé styles. It was also the 700 that got BMW a reputation for agile sporting success in the sixties, drivers such as multiple Le Mans winner Jacky Ickx commencing their careers in the 100mph competition 700s.

BMW's modern market strength stems from the September 1961-displayed, February 1962-produced, Neue Klasse 1500. In this long-awaited mid-range contender were the key features on which the BMW revival has been conducted, many of which live on today. For example the 1500 had an immensely strong single overhead camshaft (SOHC) power unit with five main bearings and an iron cylinder block, fundamentally the same as the legendary cast iron casing that has to withstand 'up to 850 horsepower in qualifying I think.' This in the

Saviour! The 4-door BMW 1500 truly began a new breed of BMW that multiplied rapidly through the sixties. Major design principles such as the independent, trailing arm, rear suspension and the slant (30°) installation of an overhead camshaft engine were established that still serve BMW, albeit in a bewildering proliferation of refined and evolutionary forms.

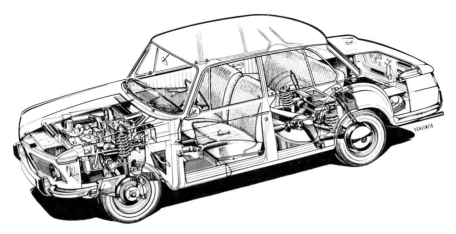

words and hands of Nelson Piquet, when mid-mounted in a 1983 Brabham BT52C, to win the World Championship.

Alex Freiherr von Falkenhausen headed the engine design team, which included the young camshaft specialist, Paul Rosche, 'father' of today's F1 and F2 racing powerplants as well as the seventies 24-valve sixes. Von Falkenhausen established the basics of combustion chamber shape allied to immense bottom end strength, and topped by an alloy head carrying chain drive for the SOHC and V-arranged valve gear that were later expanded into the six cylinder motors of the type that have powered both BMW coupés and saloons since 1968. Indeed, if you look at the bore and stroke dimensions for the successful 1990cc BMW SOHC four and its 2985cc cousin used in designs as varied as 3.0 coupés and saloons (plus the US Federal 5-Series; BMW 530i) you discover

Considerably modified today, but the independent rear suspension layout via trailing arms and upright, coil sprung, telescopic dampers remains at the heart of all the mid-eighties production BMWs, including the 6-Series. This is the 1500 original.

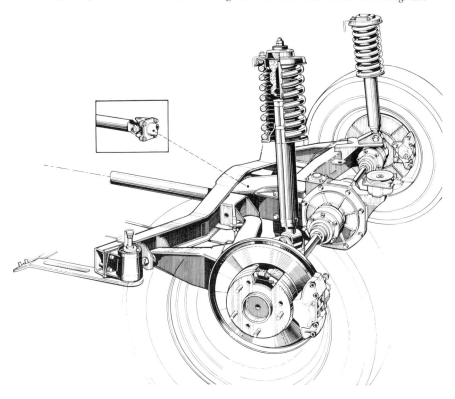

Key men in the design of the 1500, who also played a significant part in BMWs before and after the war were (left to right) Wilhelm Hofmeister (body design director who worked for 33 years at BMW prior to his May 1977 retirement; he died the following year); Fritz Fiedler (1949-64 Design & Development Chief) stands next to Eberhard Wolff and engines exponent/motorsport chief Alex Freiherr von Falkenhausen, responsible for leading the development work on both four and six cylinder overhead camshaft BMW designs that are still used today.

that short stroke of 80mm (compared to an 89mm bore) is shared between them. Cast through other BMW post-sixties four and six cylinder engines and you find all sorts of common permutations, particularly on cylinder bore, that pointer to inherent basic strength and adaptability in the original design

BMW also utilise common machine tooling for blocks, and bore sizes frequently coincide: today's 528, 728 and 628 fuel injection motors utilise that 80mm stroke, whilst the US 733/633i, and the old 730/630/530, plus the current European 732i/Turbo 745i, share that 89mm bore.

19

A 1500 in 1961 prototype form, and proud to carry the BMW trademarks, including the rear side window 'hook' and the kidney front grille. Nearly 24,000 were made before production ceased in 1964 and a complete family, including a coupé cousin, were spawned from its clean cut coachwork.

Also celebrating 50 years are this 1929 BMW 3|15 Dixi and the 1979 BMW M1, seen at the Olympiapark opposite BMW's HQ. The 160mph roadgoing M1 would donate its powerplant for further development in the 1984-produced M635 coupé.

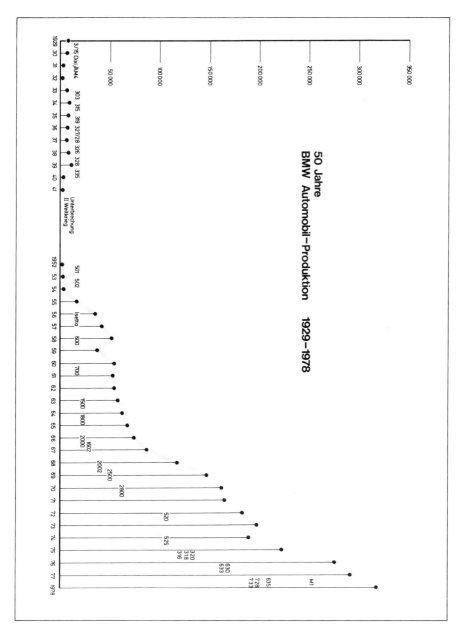

BMW production at Eisenach was small scale stuff compared with postwar; note the continuous growth from 1960 onward in this 50 year record celebration graph produced in 1979. By 1983 BMW were handsomely over the 400,000pa barrier and looking for another manufacturing plant.

We went back to Munich and the 22-floor four cylinder building (constructed in 1973) with a British-based 635 CSi and Munich's M635 to delve into the history behind 6-Series.

So the 1500 four cylinder engine, uprated to 80bhp at 5700rpm and allowing the four door 1962 1500 up to 92mph, started a BMW breed of engine that lived strongly into the eighties.

This, owing to the changing motoring environment, brought BMW into diesel turbo production and a new seventies range of small sixes tailored for the 3- and 5-Series: these compact designs can be instantly recognised from the original chain-driven SOHC engine, because they have belt-drive.

The 1500 also established BMW basics such as front engine rear drive in alliance with a trailing arm rear suspension and MacPherson front struts. In those days a mixed disc and drum brake system was the norm, along with worm and roller steering: today's 6-Series owner will have recirculating ball power steering, by ZF. Full four wheel disc braking only arrived on the pre-6-Series coupés of the seventies.

For BMW the 1500 was the most important model in the recovery, spawning a line of fleet four cylinders that escalated into the two-door (02) saloons from March 1966. These 02s took running gear like the twin carburettor/120bhp four cylinder engine developed for 1800 TI four door saloon, and ran them to greater effect in a lighter and cheaper body. American influence is always credited with pushing BMW into the classic 02 alliance of the 1990cc/100bhp single carburettor engine in the two door body (2002), but given BMW's trait of inserting just about every engine in all possible model lines, it seems unlikely that Munich would have neglected such a ploy, even if US emission laws made 2002 a logical and supremely enjoyable cohabitation. The 2002 kept on multiplying with increasing ferocity. The well balanced 2002 TI with 120bhp and 115mph (not for UK) led to the exciting Kugelfischer injection 2002 Tii and then Europe's first production turbo car, the 'wham-bam-thank-you-Mam' 2002 turbo. This generated 170bhp, if you kept it round 6000rpm, and even in 1983 I found one that would deliver most of its original shattering 130mph pace and astonishing 0-60mph acceleration in 7 seconds or so.

For our coupé story more importance can be attached to some rare low run production models of the sixties. In the next chapter we explore how these led logically into today's 6-Series as 'Born Again BMW' hurtled to proudly independent prosperity.

Chapter Two

The Big BMW Coupés:
A Tradition of Elegant Speed

A BMW purist might opt for the pre-World War II coachwork coupés wrought by specialists such as Wendler at Reutlingen on the 328 chassis/running gear as the true beginning of the BMW badge, in association with a sporty two door design offering that little bit extra in terms of flowing line allied to exceptional performance. To the author's mind a more realistic starting point for analysing the sources from which today's 6-Series sprang lies in the post-war car manufacturing activities at Munich, rather than the now East German town of Eisenach. Inevitably, to illuminate our styling research there is an Italian in the story, but you also find a Paris-domiciled Frenchman and a now retired BMW chief engineer, Bernhard Osswald, who dominated the practical production engineering of BMW between 1965 and 1975.

There are many other influences behind today's seductive 6-Series, but first we should perhaps point out that coupés built on production saloon basics–usually at least the floorpan and as many mechanical components as possible from elsewhere in a manufacturer's range–are an especially strong feature of the German motoring scene. In BMW terms there was a two door derivative of the 30 horsepower flat twin 700 from 1959 onward, the Michelotti of Turin coupé *pre*-dating the saloon by a year, and it is normal German practice to offer sharp coupé lines as an alternative to practically every saloon on the market. To illustrate just how far they have been along this alley, you may remember that even Ford's original Granada, and Taunus/Cortina, had coupé derivatives . . .

Back at BMW we recall that the fifties saw some dramatic two doors, but with a more overt Chevrolet Corvette sporting two seater style, in the Goertz-penned manner. The 503 and 507 used the separate chassis

The 328's sporting performances and mechanical fortitude left a heritage that was not forgotten after the war. Here is the 328 in its heyday, at the Nurburgring in 1938, with 328s filling all the forward rows. Car 10, closest to the camera, won at an average 75.7mph for Paul Greifzu in this supporting event to that year's German GP. Note SS insignia and number plate for competitor 19, alongside Greifzu.

and all-aluminium encased 90° V8 engine of the contemporary saloons, plus much of the running gear such as the unique steering, gearbox and basic suspension. In the latter case the rear end of the 507 was further modified with Panhard rod and location links to suit a machine that could be geared for a maximum speed of any where between 118 and 137mph.

Although 503 and 507 were very rare beasts, the principle of the larger sporting V8 BMW was carried on into the sixties by the 3200 CS coupé. Built on the same 2835mm/111.6inch wheelbase as 503 (507 was considerably shortened), the 3200 CS was significant. Not for a then considerable 160bhp at 5600rpm from eight cylinders, twin Zenith 36mm carburettors, set up on the highest compression ratio ever offered for the V8 (9:1), but for its styling.

As for the 1500 Neue Klasse four door, Munich enlisted the help of Turin's oldest current coachbuilder: Bertone. Founded in 1907 and run

Compared to the pre-war 328, the little 700 coupé was not an outright winner, but it was still a very popular mount for national German races at the Nurburgring and trained many famous names . . .

today by the son of the founder, Bertone in the late fifties and early sixties was home for a new major influence in Italian automotive haute couture: Giorgetto Giugiaro. In 1959, at the age of 21, Giugiaro became the chief stylist at Bertone, a post about as influential on automotive design trends as becoming chief engineer was at VW during the Golf's gestation . . .

From 1959-65, Giugiaro's Bertone reign under the shrewd guidance of Nuccio Bertone produced over 20 serious prototype or production cars. Best known were the 1963 Alfa Romeo Giulia Sprint coupé and Fiat's 850 (later 903-engined) coupé, both of which were produced in considerable numbers and exerted a strong influence over later 'updates' of their basic lines, or coupés from rival manufacturers.

In the earliest days of his stay, Giugiaro and the Turin team drew, and had manufactured in prototype trim, the 3200. Originally they had

The 503 was also a comparatively rare BMW V8 sports coupé, with just 412 made between the 1955 prototype and the 1959 close of production. It used the 3168cc V8 in the 140bhp twin carburettor tune.

The 501 brought BMW back into car production from a site previously more attuned to BMW aero engine and motorcycle manufacture, its smooth lines hiding a separate chassis and rugged running gear that would later form the basis for BMW coupés and sports cars.

Perhaps the most dramatic of the Graf Goertz-penned sports machines, the 507 used a shortened chassis and a 150 horsepower version of the BMW V8. Capable of 137mph on suitable gearing, the 507 was one of the rarest of all BMWs, with 253 made between 1956-59.

both coupé and cabriolet (convertible) prototypes, but only the coupé was made – and then in the usual restricted volume.

The significance to the eighties was in the creation of a large coupé with exceptionally uncluttered lines, an extraordinary amount of cabin glass, and the emphasis on the BMW family look that is basic in the styling/marketing philosophy in Munich, Graf Goertz had dared to drop the BMW *Nieren*, or kidney-style grille that has existed in one form or another since the thirties, for the 507. Yet Bertone emphasised the tradition at the front and created that curved 'hook' to the side rear window that runs throughout BMW models today with the 6-Series as no exception. Look back and you can see the same 'reverse dog leg,' antithesis to fifties American front windscreen pillar shapes, upon the similarly uncluttered panelwork of the 1500.

Only three BMW CS coupés were constructed in the Frankfurt Show debut year of 1961, and only another 535 were made before production of the last V8 BMW ceased in 1965. However, this 3300lb/124mph coupé, with its early (for BMW) use of front disc brakes, was far more significant than its production run.

To replace 3200 CS BMW reached far more into their own resources, although the end product was to owe something to today's 6-Series bodyshell manufacturing practice, in that it was constructed by Karmann at Osnabruck, 373 miles north of BMW's Dingolfing factory.

The new BMW coupés – the 2000 CS and 2000 C – appeared in June 1965 to replace the 3200 CS and marked the beginning of a new, and still current, method of coupé construction for the company. For the single carburettor C and twin carburettor CS utilised unitary steel construction, rather than the separate ladder chassis era of 501/2-related saloons and coupés, and that the steel structure was based on a current saloon (1800 Neue Klasse 4-door) and made by Karmann at Osnabruck.

Although the cabin area with acres of glass and the inevitable side rear window curve faithfully echoed the Bertone Giugiuaro style, BMW's own in-house specialist Wilhelm Hofmeister ensured the car had a completely individual model look that was always controversial. At the

Graf Goertz with the 507 in a snowy Munich of the fifties.

The 3200 CS was the last of the big V8 BMWs, ending production in 1965 when 603 had been made. The Italian lines gave a hint of the cleanly executed classic coupés to come . . .

front it had 'chinese' eyes in the form of wrap-around headlamps for most markets (many British examples simply had quad lamps). At the back the lamps were superbly blended into the metalwork in a fashion that was to last BMW a full ten years, as was the pillarless (again a Bertone echo) side window treatment.

At this stage BMW were still firmly in their four or twin cylinder motor car era, and it must be said that the 2000 coupés did not earn universal gasps of admiration for their performance, which was inevitably some way adrift of the previous beefy 3.2 litre V8s. The 2000 C/CS marked the company's first use of a full production 2-litres (89×80mm = 1990cc), providing 100bhp with a single 40mm Solex carburettor and 120bhp at 5500rpm with the 9.3:1cr, twin 40mm sidedraught carburated model. These power figures and dimensions would be most familiar to the public in the 2002/2002 TI series.

Within the 1200kg/2640lb C/CS models the single carburettor BMW power plant would give a 107mph maximum speed, with 13 seconds needed to plod the 2000C from rest to 62mph: there was an automatic transmission option that was slower still and returned just over 20mpg. But the twin carburettor CS layout cheered BMW post-'65 performance a little: say 0-62mph in 12 seconds and a 115mph maximum, but it was debatable whether they were really any faster than the 1966-68 2000 TI four door cousins, or the 1966-72 2000, despite their overtly sporting

30

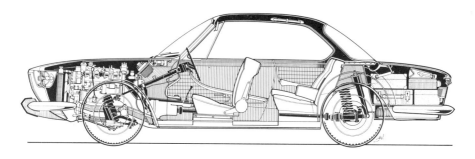

The slant four was a very tight fit inside the 2000 C/CS series, and BMW had to virtually redesign, as well as restyle, the front before presenting the six cylinder successor.

America and the first post-war BMW coupés to be produced in quantity went together naturally. Around 10,000 of the 2000 CS model with its twin carburettor engine of four cylinders were made, according to BMW.

31

Coupé 2000's elegant rear quarters with flush-fitted tail and indicator lights survived into the six cylinder series and 10 years in production.

heritage. In fact BMW's hot shot of the period was the homologation saloon racer, 1800 TI/SA (usually given as tisa) whose 1964-65 limited run extracted 130bhp at 6100rpm as the basis of competition performance from its 1773cc (84 × 80mm) BMW slant four cylinder engine. Complete with twin 45mm Weber DCOE sidedraught carburettors, this machine would launch itself from rest to 60mph in just nine seconds, and was very much the Bavarian answer to the Ford Lotus Cortinas then capering over all and sundry in the European Touring Car Championship (ETCC).

We said the C/CS coupés were built on the 1800 floorpan and this was reflected in the use of MacPherson strut front suspension and a trailing arm rear end, with a mixed disc and drum braking system. The 2550mm/100.4inch wheelbase and front/rear track figures of 1330mm/52.4inches and 1375mm/54.2inches were also shared between coupés and the 1800 saloons, or the later 2000 four doors, for that matter.

The 2000 coupés were phased out in 1969, when it could be seen that the improved performance twin carburettor CS had attracted most business with 9999 produced as against just 2837 for the 2000C.

From September 1968 onward it was public knowledge as to what recipe BMW had concocted to carry their coupé ambitions into the seventies. For the six cylinder 2500 and 2800 saloons were announced, with the 2800 CS coupé cousin produced at Karmann from December that year. There was no 2500 counterpart in the coupé range until the 1974-75 fuel crisis model was needed.

So the 2800 CS, carrying perhaps the sweetest six cylinder engine that BMW produce (a unit that lives in the eighties with fuel injection) began a new BMW coupé legend that was to be really hard for any successor to emulate. In retrospect this was slightly surprising as the 2800 CS was far from thoroughbred. Although BMW had now developed the family look with extraordinary success, so that the coupé and saloon 2800 were clearly on kissing cousin terms, the 2800 CS used a reworked version of the 2-litre Karmann coupé bodywork, rather than a chopped down derivative of the new 1968 six cylinder saloons. Similar illusions tie together 6-Series and 7 in the public mind today, but the basic 6-Series floorpan is that of 5-Series, rather than the visually similar 7-Series.

To insert the six cylinder engine in what amounted to a 2000C/CS from the front windscreen pillar rearward, involved a substantial and beneficial redesign. Overall length went from 4530mm/178.3inches to 4630mm/182.3inches, most of that extra four inches devoted to prising in the still 30° slant six cylinder engine block. Wheelbase and track were increased compared to the 2-litre coupés too: 2800 CS rode on a 2625mm/103.4inches, a three inch stretch of the original. It had a front/rear track measurement of 1446mm/56.9inches and 1402mm/55.1inches, that near five inch front expansion reflecting the installation of the six cylinder car's front struts and disc brakes, along with 6J × 14 steel wheels in initial German production. At the rear the 2800 CS continued with the 250mm rear drum brakes (9.8in.) that traced back to 1500, those front 272mm/10.7inch discs of the usual non-ventilated type of the period, and also familiar in other BMW applications.

The six cylinder 2800 CS naturally displayed a weight gain at 1355 kg/2981lb, but it was more than offset by the power of the 86 × 80mm twin downdraught Zenith carburated 2788cc. At 6000rpm there was another 50hp (170 total) available from the engine, and that was accompanied by a substantial 172lb.ft of torque at 3700rpm. Enough to carry that big two door coupé toward 130mph – the factory recorded 128mph; *Motor* magazine confirmed exactly that figure. The factory only reckoned on 10 seconds for 0-62mph, but that was over-modest; *Motor* made it 8.5 seconds for 0-60mph and many others concurred.

Elongated and more graceful than ever, the six cylinder coupé was produced from 1968 to 1975. This alloy wheeled example is equipped with the 3-litre carburettor engine. Made between 1971 and 1975, the 3.0 CS possessed 180bhp and a maximum speed of nearly 130mph.

Anywhere around 20mpg was typical for hard-driven 2.8 litre coupés, the factory their usual pessimistic selves and forecasting 17.1mpg, which was more likely for the slower automatic. Anywhere from 19 to 23mpg over British terrain appeared normal.

The carburated 2.8 sold nearly the same total as both 2000 C/CS had managed, around 9500 in its three season life, before it followed the saloons up the enlarged engine three litre path in 1971. Just as important as the 89 × 80mm (née 2-litre four) dimensions for 2985cc and an extra 10hp (180bhp at 6000rpm), was the adoption of four wheel 272mm/10.7 ventilated disc brakes. The chassis behaviour of the 2800 CS was more usually criticised for an inferiority to contemporary BMW saloons – which were built from scratch rather than converted designs, as had been the coupé case. Given the capability of those disc brakes and the sheer speed of 3.0 CS it was nice to be able to slow before things got completely out of hand . . .

As the 2800 CS had not been available in the UK until October 1969, it was not surprising to find that the 1971-introduced 3.0 CS, as discussed, and its fuel-injection (Bosch D-Jetronic) brother of 1971 took until January 1972 and May of the same year (3.0 CSi) to permeate the UK.

The 3.0 CSi with its slightly uprated 9.1:1cr, instead of the usual 2.8/3.0 ratio of 9:1, plus the fuel injection equipment, was rated with 200bhp at 5500rpm – saving 500rpm over the carburated coupé's power peak. Also a meaty 200lb.ft. of torque at 4300rpm was available, versus the 3.0 CS on 188lb.ft. at 3700rpm. The 3.0 Si/CSi was a quick car in saloon or coupé style: BMW reported 136mph and 0-62mph in 8 seconds. British road testers found that the car ran out of steam at just over 130mph, but there were a few who recorded high 7-second acceleration times for 0-60mph. Fuel consumption still hovered around the 20mpg mark if the car was driven with restraint, but hard testing use saw closer to 16-17mpg overall.

The same pillarless coupé accommodated six cylinder engines from 2.5 litres/150bhp to 3153cc/206bhp, emphasising the versatility BMW demand from their straightforward designs.

However, it was not the commercially-enduring 3.0 CS and CSi machines of 1971-75 that attracted most public attention and ensured that the early seventies BMW coupés became such a source of inspired collector bidding in the eighties. Yet they did provide the bulk of the profitable 44,254 coupés BMW sold between 1968-75, as opposed to 252, 559 six cylinder saloons made and sold in the same period.

No, public attention was directed at a new big BMW derivative that peaked its limited production nose into the LHD-only world during 1971. To further their saloon car racing ambitions BMW made a lot of moves in the 1971-73 period. Priority One was made the CSL, L for the German equivalent of Lightweight, and meaning in practical terms the wide use of alloy panels, where today's specials plump for Kevlar and other High Tech composite materials.

The first CSLs were seen in the Germany of 1971, but they were not

The supreme expression of the 1968-75 BMW coupé series was the racing basis provided by this near-140mph 3.0 CSL of 1973. Complete with 3.2 litre injected six, such machines were the fastest BMWs in the seventies range and went on winning motor races long after production had ceased.

recognised in time to make any difference to BMW racing fortunes during 1972, until BMW had also acquired the Ford Cologne men who were the driving forces behind the Capri's success in lightweight Ford-Weslake fuel injection V6 trim. The key personnel were former Cologne Competitions manager and ex-Porsche long distance team works driver Jochen Neerpasch, who oversaw the development of BMW Motorsport (it was a separate company: BMW Motorsport GmbH) Neerpasch was supported by, and left all the engineering expertise, outside Paul Rosche's traditional engine brief, to Martin Braungart, another Ford refugee bored by the Capri's domination as a racing saloon versus a series of modified road cars. The duo brought with them, for the 1973 season, Hans Joachim Stuck, possibly the man who typifies BMW in touring car races above all others to US and British spectators. Although Austrian Dieter Quester had won BMW European titles four times, including the 1983 last round victory against Jaguar, when the keep-fit fanatic and Herr Falkenhausen's son-in-law, was 44 years old!

Together with the presence of a man who would go on to scale the managerial heights of Ford of Europe and the parent company in the USA, Bob Lutz, this led to BMW becoming far more aggressive about their sporting ambitions, and led to another significant strand in the BMW coupé reputation.

The CSL started as merely a lighter CS with a shared 2985cc carburettor 180bhp power plant, but lightweight panels (including the easily-scarred doors), special seats, sports three spoke steering wheel and $7J \times 14$ alloy wheels with 195/70 VR radials–the latter from Michelin on the example I tried for *Motor Sport* in their July 1972 issue. Quoted weight for a 3.0 CS had risen to 1400kg/3080lb by this stage, the CSL credited with 200kg/440lb less, which was worth a whole second off the 0-62mph acceleration time, plus a mysteriously gained 2mph on maximum speed (134mph).

When Neerpasch *et al* arrived and started lighting fires under the private ambitions of BMW performance specialists Alpina and Schnitzer with a hefty bonus scheme, whilst quickening the pace of large coupé development, the CSL scheme really took off. Actually what confounded Ford was that the coupé would no longer take off from race track curves or crests after this intensive development.

The second stage in CSL development was the 1972/early 1973 model with a slightly oversize (3003cc) version of the fuel injected engine that differed only from the 2985cc unit discussed earlier in an 0.25mm extra diameter for the bore to give 89.25 × 80mm. Power, 200bhp, the 9.5:1cr, and maximum torque of fractionally over 200lb.ft. were all unaffected. Weight was up by 70kg to 1270kg/2794lb, but the sole purpose of this model was to ensure that BMW could race with an engine capacity over 3-litres, whereas the rival Capris were still stuck below this capacity. BMW Motorsport started the 1973 racing season with a 3191cc version of the straight six engine (92 × 80mm) that gave up to 340bhp at 7800rpm. This was a little bit more than the Capri V6 could provide after years of development and the fitment of unique alloy Weslake cylinder heads, but still the BMWs had a considerable weight disadvantage–the Ford being homologated for racing at under 1000kg! Soon BMW Motorsport had a 3331cc engine able to race as a result of

Batmobile! You can see where the nickname came from in this study of the 1973 CSL, displaying the front wing strakes, rear window hoop and complex air dam/tailplane layout. All were developed very quickly by a Munich team hungry for saloon car racing success. It worked . . .

that oversize 3003cc roadgoing CSL. This Kugelfischer fuel injected unit usually raced with an 11.2:1cr and up to 366bhp at a maximum 8200rpm for its 94 × 80mm dimensions.

Still Paul Rosche and the Motorsport team wanted more cubic inches, but that was only part of the story for the CSL in its final form. Working with the aid of a short session in the Stuttgart High School wind tunnel, and a racing CSL as a guinea pig, Martin Braungart and his cohorts produced a fantastic aerodynamic wing set for the racing BMW. In order that it should be recognised for racing as from July 1st 1973, a series of road cars had to be produced and these ultimate CSLs also carried the longer stroke six cylinder engine. With an 89.25mm bore and an 84mm stroke the road power unit was uprated with 206bhp at 5600rpm from 3153cc. More importantly in road and race terms, torque was also increased: for the road car there was 211lb.ft at 4200rpm, whilst the racers were bored to a full 94 × 84mm for 3496cc and would provide

In 1975 BMW went racing with CSL coupés carrying these 3.5 litre sixes containing 24 valves, two overhead camshafts and an awesome 430 DIN bhp at 8500rpm. The power unit, here mounted at the traditional slant for racing in the USA, but also used vertically in 1976 and passed onto the M1 mid-engine car, was the forerunner of today's M635 powerplant.

370bhp plus lashings of torque with a slightly lower power peak (8000rpm) than the 3.3 litre predecessor.

Certainly this 370bhp helped win races against Fords that were unlikely to have more than 320bhp, but it was the 'Batmobile' wing system that demoralised all shred of opposition. Braungart and company came up with a deep front spoiler used in alliance with front bonnet strakes (still sold by Irmscher for GM products, and many other makes!), a hoop over the rear screen and an enormous rear wing with two vertical blades, a transverse aeleron and a bootlid spoiler. Braungart confided that the front and rear spoilers, plus the wing, were the vital components, providing such downforce on their own account that BMW could frequently run softer compound tyres than the opposition. The advantage of such a wing system over a Capri with a front spoiler only (not even a 'ducktail' was homologated for the Ford's bootlid until the 1974 season), can be imagined, especially around the Nurburgring's hilly curves. For July 1973's edition of the Nurburgring 6 hours both Ford and BMW pulled out all the GP names they could find, Alpina – BMW running a then BRM GP driver, Niki Lauda. The eighties McLaren Formula One ace then pulled out pole position for the Alpina CSL, setting a time of 8 minutes 17.3 seconds against 8 minutes 23.0 seconds for the fastest Ford, which was the machine for Jochen Mass, rather than two of the world's quickest men at the time, who were also co-opted into the Ford fold: Jackie Stewart and Emerson Fittipaldi. So the wings worked well, right from their debut, and Ford were destined not to win another European Championship round that season . . .

The road version of the last CSL had the 3.2 litre engine mentioned, plus plastics for most of the additional aero kit and the usual aluminium lightweight panels. Again weight was quoted at 1270kg, but it should be noted that the British importers ordered 500 CSLs of considerably more luxurious specification that usually lacked the items like alloy-skinned door panels that Karmann normally included in a CSL build. I say normally as inspection of a pristine example owned by a Kentish BMW dealer of a CSL supplied directly from the importer of the period (then a private concession in the UK: BMW took over in January 1980) showed all sorts of deviations from accepted CSL equipment. Even during a casual inspection items like electrification for rear window operation, but handles up front, swiftly showed that concours judges of originality will have a problem in the UK!

The road 3.2 litre CSL came with the usual spats over the wheelarches, rather than the huge wheelarch extensions favoured by racers, and thus popular for road cars of subsequent decades. The standard wheel was a 7J × 14inch alloy type with 195/70 VR radial tyres. The interior was upgraded as before with sports front seats and a rather more dashing design of steering wheel, but the 10.7inch vented disc brakes and ZF Gemmer worm and roller steering remained as for lesser production coupés.

Performance of the later big-engined CSLs was considerable: 0-60mph occupied a scant 7 seconds and top speed was usually recorded as 138mph without the wings, or slightly over 140mph with the wing kit installed. I make the distinction because German market cars were delivered with the wing kit in the boot as they were not recognised for road use in BMW's home country!

Racing for recognition in the USA, BMW's CSL coupés (this one driven by Hans Joachim Stuck jnr) carried the Bavarian Motor Works message loud and clear to those who thought the B stood for British!

The CSL's official production span was until 1975, but it lived on as a racer in Group 2 and Group 5 after its production demise. Unusually even the factory ran these obsolete machines in 1976, whilst privateers carried on with the 3.5 litre racing motor and the full wing kit to win European Touring Car Championship titles until 1979.

In racing guise the big BMW coupé was extremely popular and very spectacular. It was the best racing saloon in terms of long-lived results that BMW have ever had, and it very nearly put one over Porsche when campaigned in 1976 Group 5 races. Work started on a four valve per cylinder M49-coded six cylinder engine in September 1973 and over 400bhp was provided immediately even by the 3.2 litre prototype. Despite the fuel crisis cutting race budgets sharply, the 24-valve M49 was debuted in two CSL's for the April Austrian European Championship round and gave Hans Joachim Stuck/Jacky Ickx a win with some 440bhp available at 8500rpm. The power unit was further developed to provide a reliable 470bhp at 9000rpm, when mounted vertically, instead of at the normal production 30° slant, with new water channeling to combat overheating and a far straighter run for the top exhaust manifolds. In such form it could be seen racing in the IMSA series within the USA, although the four valve engine was not usually mounted vertically in that series, as that answer was the result of a 1975-76 development programme. The full benefits of vertical engine mounting became apparent in 1976 when BMW supported the efforts of three well financed teams in Group 5 CSLs to take on Porsche, and fielded their own development car. This was the ultimate CSL. Coded M49/4 the engine thundered forth 750 to 800bhp from 3191cc in race trim, and was equipped with KKK turbocharging. It only raced three times, notably in the hands of the late Ronnie Peterson, but was perhaps the most sensational saloon a manufacturer has ever fielded with the ability to fry the driver's feet and produce strong acceleration wheelspin in third gear, with flames to delight the onlookers throughout!

Whilst the turbo did not lead to any great BMW production quest in itself – the 3210cc turbo 745i is a very different (256bhp) luxury saloon – the four valve six cylinder unit had become increasingly important since the CSL and cousins ceased their elegant road and track performances.

For, as we shall see, the four valve six became the basis for the M88 production equivalent for the M1 supercar. That led to a 6-Series

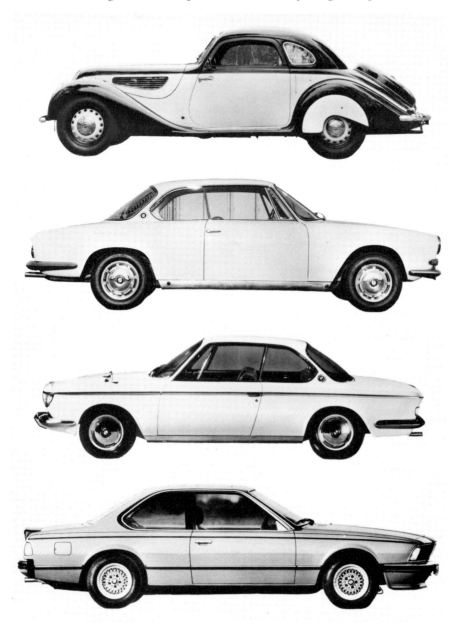

BMW coupé tradition commemorated by (top to bottom): the 80bhp version of the 328 engine within this graceful thirties 327/28; the sixties 3200 CS with V8 power; the 1965-68 2000 C/CS and the 635 CSi of 1978 onward.

sporting such a 24 valve power plant in 1983, but with a powerplant updated in many detail respects over the original mid-engined M1 application. Unfortunately there does not seem to be a racing opening for the unit in M635 in 1984, but the spirit that made the 6-Series such a prestigiously important introduction to BMW can clearly be understood from the astonishing and long lived versatility of the 1968–75 coupés.

Now we see how BMW engineers and stylists laboured to try and follow such an effective coupé act!

Chapter Three

Conception of a Coupé Classic

During the opening years of the seventies' decade there were a number of widely differing influences within BMW that moulded the final form of the 6-Series coupés. The most obvious inputs to the latest large BMW coupé were those of Parisian styling chief Paul Bracq and the practical engineering of BMW's top technician in the 1965-75 era, Bernhard Osswald. Yet we also have to recall the effect of the 1973/74 fuel crisis, and the politics surrounding the importation of BMWs into the USA, which was to assume its export market leadership, thus becoming vital in any BMW long term planning. From a practical engineering viewpoint BMW's facilities were getting better all the time, although they lacked their own wind tunnel test facility until the eighties. By 1975 the BMW proving ground at Ismaning, just north of Munich and off the route that would take one to Audi at Ingolstadt, was completed. However, it was obvious from the safety viewpoint and in mechanical development that Ismaning had already played a significant role in 6-Series development.

The American situation revolved around the vigorous importer Max Hoffman. The American-based Austrian had brought BMWs into America since 1950 and, by 1973, was selling some 13,700 a year. Hoffman is often credited with the idea of uniting the 2-litre BMW four cylinder and the 02 shell to create the BMW 2002, and it was obvious that he certainly ensured BMW never overlooked the unique conditions – such as stringent emission and crash protection standards – that ruled American sales potential.

In line with the usual pattern of manufacturers taking over profitable overseas importation operations–and provoked by Max Hoffman's high profile personality – BMW began a legal bout with Hoffman, from which they emerged with ownership rights and a new company: BMW

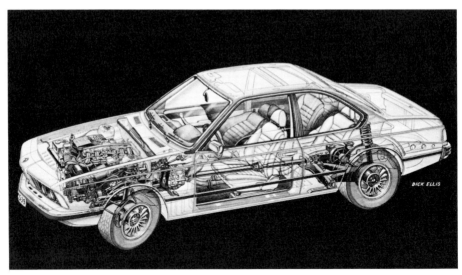

6-Series laid bare: BMW were so proud of this Dick Ellis drawing that they presented it to visitors as part of a quartet of fine cutaways by differing artists.

North America. That was in 1974. By 1977 BMW was hitting close to 30,000 sales in the USA. In 1982, when America had still to fully recover from the recession, BMW North America at Montvale NJ reported the sale of an astonishing 52,000 units. 'Astonishing' because the American car market as a whole was down 6 per cent and BMW were up a solid 25 per cent!

To put the export markets in perspective the company accounts show the following BMW subsidiary sales during 1982: BMW (GB) Ltd, 23,000 representing a 34 per cent gain over the previous year, and an equally astounding 70 per cent gain in numbers over the days of privately owned BMW Concessionaires. BMW Italia shifted more units, but they tended to be the less profitable 3-Series mix, owing to the economy and punitive taxes on larger cars like 6-Series: in 1982 the Italians took 28,700 BMWs, down 17 per cent on 1981. In France, 3-Series cars also provided an increase in numbers, to 33,500, but here the 6 and 7-Series held their profitable ground, although the percentage of larger and more luxuriously equipped BMWs gravitated toward Great Britain, the USA and the Arab states. Naturally Switzerland offers a good home for new BMWs and they show the highest percentage ownership of BMW cars in Europe with 4.4 per cent of the total market, some 12,800 BMWs in 1982. Exotic locations showed BMW's increasing acceptance worldwide, with a 45 per cent sales gain to 5300 units by BMW Japan Corp. in Tokyo and 2400 BMWs sold by BMW Australia Ltd. in Melbourne.

Thus we can see that American legislation was entirely relevant when BMW began penning and developing a new coupé. A design that, owing to its comparatively low sales volume, would be expected to last BMW well into the eighties, perhaps a full ten years with suitable facelifts.

Most relevant amongst American laws affecting the 6-Series we see today, compared with what might have been, were those governing crash tests, in particular the inverted drop designed to probe roof crush-resistance. Such tests deterred BMW from importing the 3.0 CS in Federal form beyond the 1974 model year. The twin carburettor American CS derivative already hampered by body weight escalating to over 3250lbs in its final year, the encumbrance of impact bumpers boosting overall length close to 190inches.

BMW knew when they set out to style a successor to the 1968 coupés that it could no longer have the pillarless side glass with elegantly slim roof pillars. Paul Bracq's concern, carried out with sophisticated skill in production, was to disguise the considerable strength of roof supports needed to pass such tests – and to guard for future legislation. This led BMW into a 6-Series that was necessarily beefier than its predecessors, for the frontal impact zones and the general crumple zone behaviour front and rear, commanded much development time and the provision 'of perhaps a little more sheet metal than we would use today. In fact some of that extra weight has been taken out in later 6-Series', in the words of one senior BMW engineering executive speaking in Munich during 1984.

Being chief stylist at BMW is not an easy job, particularly if you are a foreigner, for the natural desire of stylists is to explore the future and get such ideas into production. Whilst BMW, like Mercedes, have carefully cultivated a conservative image for their appearance with strong 'family' ties.

Writing in the mid–eighties, when ex-Audi British stylist Martin Smith had been to BMW, and back outside with even greater speed than Bracq managed in his seventies tenure, one could see that BMW's biggest headache was not contemporary. Sales of all BMW models, particularly the conservatively revamped 5-Series and smaller 3-Series cousin were at record levels in 1984 – but setting a new family look for the late eighties and early nineties, was a considerable challenge.

In 1972 Paul Bracq gave us his vision of BMW's future with the construction of a mid-engined, gullwing, 2-litre prototype with a distinct wedge theme and wide use of deformable materials front and rear that would regain their original shape after slight impacts. The BMW Turbo prototype proved a crowd-stopper at the Autumn round of motor shows and a second example of the transversely-engined Turbo was made at Michelotti: the first example can be seen in the BMW Museum at Munich.

Only broad themes could be lifted from this extreme show car – although it is as well to recall that BMW would be selling an Italo-Germanic mid-engined hybrid two seater by the close of the seventies (M1) – of which the most obvious in the 6-Series was the use of the

Paul Bracq's influence was at its strongest in the BMW gullwing show cars of 1972/3. The strong downward sweep of the nose was also allowed, in much less striking style, to permeate the original 6-Series front. Styling drawings of the same period show 6-Series with retractable headlamps but otherwise recognisable coupé lines.

bonnet vee (also a feature of other production BMWs by the time the 6 was seen) and the strong bias toward a downswept nose. The usual coupé themes of a large glass area for the cabin, plus the use of a long bonnet line were blended into existing trademarks such as the BMW grille outline and the rear window line. The quadruple headlamp front end was tied firmly to the 7-Series saloon that would make its debut in 1977. When it came to facelift time in the eighties, both saloon and coupé shared a softer common theme for the front end.

What is in a name?

Internally, as for many mechanical components, the new BMW coupé owed much to the 5-Series 4-door saloons of 1972. Direct replacements for the sixties 4-door 1800/2000 series that had set BMW back on the

The 1972 5-Series cockpit brought the BMW single viewing pane instrument layout, a wide use of rotary controls – such as for the heater, on the centre console (bracketing the analogue clock with its ingenious rotary fan speed control) – and generally previewed the 'command centre' ergonomics that are used in further refined form for the eighties BMWs.

middle class road to prosperity, the 520 pioneered a new, logical, and still retained, approach to model designations and driver-control layout.

Thus the 5 opening to the model number indicated 5-Series and '20' revealed the capacity in litres. In 6-Series today you have 628 with 2.8 litres through to M635 in which there is a $3\frac{1}{2}$ litre engine. If you are finnicky there are minor deviations from the rules in the BMW line. Most obvious is the 3.2 litre 745i: here the logic is that the turbocharged 3.2 litre is equivalent to a cylinder capacity of 4.5 litres, using the international touring car turbo multiplication formula of 1.4! In the 6-Series there is only slight deviation from the truth: the post-Summer 1982 down-sizing of the engine within 635 should have brought with it a 634 badge . . . A 633 should be a 632, as for 732, as they both use 3210cc motivation.

Aside from the numerals, BMW prefixes and suffixes are all internationally accepted, though you might think that M in front of M635 was for Munich rather than Motorsport, the department who conceived and largely developed M1, M535i and M635i. The CS suffix simply defined Coupé Sport in the sixties as opposed to plain C for coupé on the single carburettor 2000 C. The 'i' is always for injection and panders to foreigners, for Mercedes stick to E for Einspritz, the German for injection. Models without the 'i' in 6-Series were confined only to some of the original launch line, these carburated coupés generally less desirable on the secondhand car market owing to inferior performance coupled to increased fuel consumption.

The cockpit layout devised by Bracq and his colleagues was later widely imitated and has only really been modified in detail in the twelve years that have elapsed since 5-Series launch. Look inside every mass production hatchback of international significance today and you are liable to find an echo of BMW's single pane viewing panel over the instrumentation. It was not a totally original thought, even then, but BMW applied it so well, with a complete lack of reflections and the clearest possible layout of large black and white dials that it became a hallmark – and high point – of their interiors. Discuss digital instrumentation with BMW engineers today and you still find an understandable reluctance to get involved with this aspect of the electronics age, although 6-Series has consistently shown that BMW do care about this aspect of a car's interior information services, starting

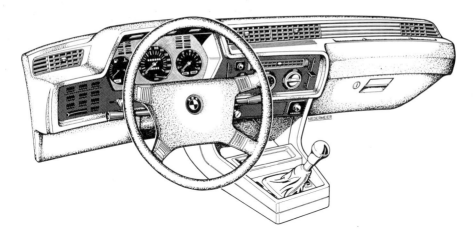

The drawing for 1976 630/633 CSi layout recalls handy placement of horn buttons within the four spoke steering wheel, clarity of three dial instrumentation layout, the lefthand location of the 7-light monitor on vital functions (since picked up by many other BMW models) and the rotary controls, like 5-Series, on the centre console. They were certainly generous with the ventilation air outlets for the fascia, but they had to be with large glass areas and less than complimentary comments from owners of earlier BMWs . . .

with the 'Active' test panel that monitored key functions on command from the driver's finger on a button. On-board computers of fabled complexity and Service Interval indicators continued BMW's preferred approach to the age of electronics, along with Robert Bosch's Motronic engine management systems for the eighties.

Instrumentation aside, the stylists created a BMW interior in the 5-Series where graceful sweeps of the fascia brought controls within a handspan or so of the driver and treated his relationship with a four spoke steering wheel (that could be adjusted for distance rather than vertical movement) very seriously. This led to the commanding position found on most BMWs, the 6-Series favouring a slightly lower stance, though still with vertical seat adjustment to provide that arms-stretched ideal that BMW favour.

Other cabin features that the 5-Series cars introduced and that would find an echo in succeeding BMWs, including the current coupé, were the rotary heater controls and the use of subdued orange-tint night illumination for instrumentation that provided just speed, rpm, water

51

The wheelbase is the same, but the clever extension of front and rear overhangs moves the 6-Series (below) into a completely different class than the square-rigged original 5-Series shown above. Note that both feature recognisable interpretations of the rear window frame curve at their edges with the back roof pillar.

temperature and fuel contents as the usual diet on all sporting BMWs. From memory the only modern BMW I can recall with an oil pressure gauge was the copiously-instrumented M1. A central clock with heavily-indented outer ring to vary ventilation fan levels was also a long term BMW cabin feature.

Detail development

A general Motors employee in the sixties, Walter Stork is the man in charge of chassis development for the BMW of the eighties, but when he arrived at BMW 'in 1970/71, I was involved in many aspects of our engineering work except that for the engine'. Then the detailing of the new coupé progressed, much along the lines of what was available from elsewhere in BMW, rather than from a clean sheet of engineering paper.

'There was no plan for any four cylinder engines, so we knew the running gear would all have to work with a six cylinder range with the object of being easy and fun to drive. Our first engineering job was to evaluate what was available from the 5-Series and from the forthcoming 7s, or the existing old six cylinder BMW lines, that would fit into this new coupé. In many cases you must remember that we were restricted by what was engineered for the 5-Series.' A key point, for the six cylinder 2.5 litre 525 was not sold until a year after the 520/520i launch in 1972. The 528, utilising the 2.8 litre engine that would be part of a later 6-Series, was not sold until 1975. We discussed engines separately, but the first 6-Series had only 3.0 and 3.3 litres.

Walter Stork recalled that an essential part of their engineering approach to the coupé was, 'to avoid components of heavier weight. The 6 was supposed to be lighter and livelier. You must remember that the same parts in a 6-Series have an easier life than those parts in a 7-Series saloon. Taking out 100 Dm was not the point in a luxury coupé; we were not trying to save money, but to save 50kg was important.' An excellent example of that approach was in the use of a 5-Series based final drive and rear axle for the coupés right up to 635, 'but when they came along with the four valve engine for the Motorsport 635, then it was too much,' said Herr Stork with a rare laugh, ' and then we did have to change the rear gear set and casing to that used on the 735 all along. In turn that meant considerably reshaping the M635's floor around that area.'

53

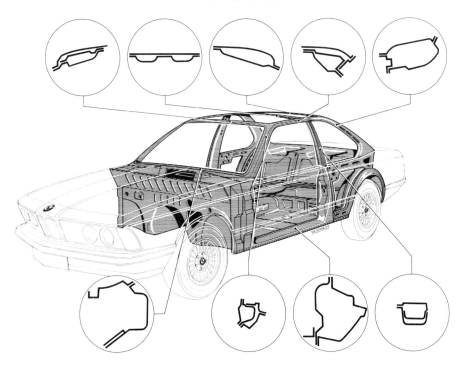

Where the extra weight came from: BMW outline the key body points and profiles that contributed to immensely improved crash and rollover safety, compared with its predecessors.

Starting from the ground floor up there was the same 2626mm/103.3inch wheelbase floorpan to rework from 5-Series to the new coupé. Herr Stork explained, 'essentially we needed to change all the bracketry for the attachment of new components, provide a new seating position with appropriate steering to wheel angle for a lower and rear-placed driving position.' Most important changes underneath were directed at ensuring six cylinder standards of braking and suspension could be attached to the 5-Series floorpan, which was obviously at the four cylinder pre-production stage when 6-Series engineering began.

Although the dimensions of the 528's brakes in 1975 and 630/633/635 discs were identical, with 280/11inch fronts and 272mm/10.7inch rears, the 528 started production life with solid discs, whereas the 6-Series had used four wheel ventilated discs in most models from its inception. The 5-Series did get ventilated front discs eventually (1977) but retains solid rears to this day. Thus the mountings for brakes and suspension on 6-

Series differed in detail, but BMW's sporting customers in racing, or at specialists such as Alpina when preparing road cars, tend to treat the two models as very similar indeed at the preparation stage. For example much of the 1982 Group A racing 528i technology, in itself having some components tracing back to the glory days of the Group 2 racing CSL, or later M1 usage, was transferred to the 1983 Group A racing version of 635 that BMW Motorsport sold so successfully in kit form during 1983/84.

On the suspension side Walter Stork has kept the BMW tradition for classic rear drive handling alive, a philosophy that has not been without controversy in a motoring world that now accepts front drive as the conventional safety wisdom. Besides which BMW have Bavarian

All dimensions are in millimetres (1mm=0.03937in.). Sharing a 5-Series wheelbase, BMW's new coupé was also built within fractions of the 1968-75 coupé's wheelbase, but was about 5 inches longer, 2.2 inches wider, marginally lower and significantly heavier.

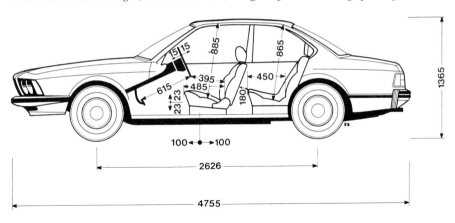

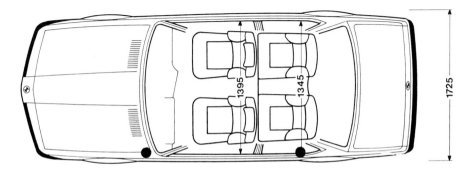

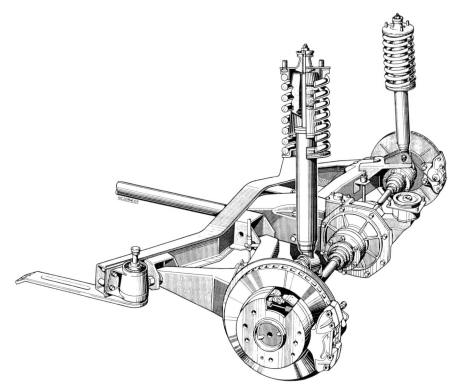

Still recognisable from its 1500 antecedents, BMW's rear trailing arm layout for the original 6-Series is instantly distinguishable by the use of ventilated rear disc brakes, which were not installed on its contemporary BMW brethren.

neighbours up at Ingolstadt to whom four wheeldrive comes naturally. Although the charming Claudi (devoted Mini driver . . . !) in BMW's press office will cheerfully tell you, 'up there is not really Bavaria at all!'

Obviously BMW's handling and roadholding principles extend throughout the present front engine rear drive range – you can still make their engineers shudder with a mention of front drive – so Herr Stork's thoughts on the matter were of more than usual interest. 'It is a conscious decision that we make, for 6-Series and the other cars in our range. It would be possible to make our cars without the power oversteer that we have, but the price is that the car has a less exact feeling. So the car has less information feedback to the driver through the steering. We let the driver decide by giving him enough information, early enough to

56

make up his mind. Drive fast on a curving road and you will see what I mean. It is dangerous under these conditions to be in a car which is always understeering, always trying to make its way off the road with the nose first! There is no way to change its course. In our cars you can ease the throttle, or have some more speed; it's up to you. With a very powerful engine it is even more important to arrange things our way. It is not a philosophy that originated with me, but just what the customers want.

'For cars on dry roads, or at least not on ice, the BMW front engine, rear drive, handling and roadholding is still a very good system. That applies for the foreseeable future, but for ice and conditions like that, yes, it must be four wheel drive (4-WD). At least it's a lot better than front drive! So you say OK to 4-WD, but then you ask yourself . . . How

At the front the 6-Series displays leading location link and separate lower arm for the MacPherson strut layout, with the ZF variable assistance steering prominent, along with the bushed roll bar twisting its way over the subframes. As at the rear, the basics would be based on the same principles, but considerable detail alterations have improved suspension behaviour considerably since 1976. Improved tyres played an important role, particularly the Michelin TRX, which BMW have supported more enthusiastically than the many manufacturers who dislike its unique tyre and wheel dimensions.

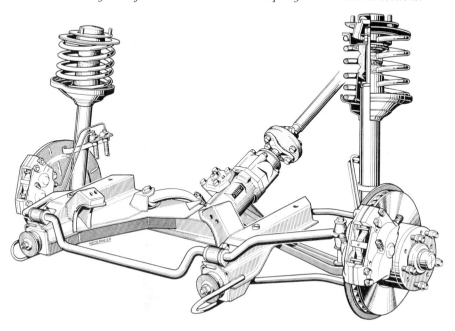

many people *really* want it? Then there is the extra cost, and sometimes the car does not feel so good.

'In the 6-Series and the later developments that became possible, such as the 7-Series double link front suspension, or the new angle for the rear trailing arms that started in 528i, we could only go as fast as production would let us.' Herr Stork reflecting on the situation where the costlier 6-Series often had to wait for the high volume products to make an engineering change economically possible.

There has been little complaint about the riding qualities of the 6-Series. For there have been various layouts tried over the years, and there has always been the option of more sporting ride/handling compromise either through specially ordered parts as a kind of Sport package, or through BMW Motorsport. Or by simply trading up to the more overtly sporting choices such as 635 with the (initial) option of TRX wheels and tyres that later became standard. Today there's the alternative of the M635, but it should be noted that the special Bilsteins and new springs supplied with this model actually provided a more absorbent ride than the TRX-shod standard 635CSi we took to Germany to provide our Munich research; sportier does not have to mean harsher!

On the ride subject Walter Stork recalled, 'we did a lot of work to match the original 6-Series spring and shock absorbers to a natural frequency with the new seating. Some of this work was completed at Ismaning, some in disguised road prototypes and we had our usual outings to the Nurburgring as well. We also have some poor roads we use in Europe, but there are not many left, so I am not going to tell you where we did such work!

'Generally we find a limitation to the gas-filled monotube shock absorber for our normal production models, so we regularly fit Boge or Fichtel and Sachs twin tube hydraulic dampers, which are able to differentiate between bump and rebound. For a sports option the gas-filled shock absorber is acceptable, but it may be that some developments going on at this time will make the compromise we need. If we use gas-filled shock absorbers, they are normally from Bilstein.

'In all cases we try to reduce the changes in track/camber and introduce more anti-dive. For the 6-Series this was only possible with higher mounting of the track control arm; the more power you have, the more anti-dive is required. The objective is always to provide the right dynamics. Not just away from the lights when the transfer of weight is a problem, but for all conditions.

'We try to give values the driver can always handle safely,' concluded Walter Stork.

Engines engineering

A quick dash to another BMW building in the suburbs of Munich—a badly needed central engineering HQ was awaited when this was written – took us to the exciting spiritual heart of any BMW, the engine development and research block. Waiting for us rather nervously was a typically long-serving BMW employee, Georg Ederer. He was apprehensive over a lack of English practice in stark contrast to the marketing/PR people, but as with all the BMW engine men, the basic enthusiasm soon overcame the initial reserve and information was soon spilling forth.

First you have to gauge the depth of commitment BMW show to engineering motor car engines, 'not lorries as well', as they ask you to remember in a passing reference to Mercedes' larger staff! There are some 760 engines engineers at Munich on the passenger car programme: BMW Motorsport employs over 100 staff and their responsibilities cover all the competition units for Grand Prix racing, as well as Formula 2 and saloon car racing, plus the detail development that went into M635, a subject we return to in a later chapter. American readers may be familiar with BMW in the turbo diesel car market, for there is an agreement with Ford US to supply the diesel six which BMW themselves use in European trim for the 524 TD. Although there is a separate development department, along with the new plant at Steyr in Austria (a wholly BMW-owned subsidiary since April 1982: originally a co-development with Steyr-Daimler-Puch AG) BMW also did practical development work for Ford in Munich – the large American Fords sometimes sprawling all over the Motorsport department – or at the Ismaning test track.

Back with our 760 engine men in Munich we find they have the use of 46 test cells 'for functional use and another 22 for durability runs.' Georg Ederer amplified, 'such testing is at least twice as hard as when I first came here in 1966. Now we normally run at least 300 hours at full, *full*, load which will probably be 6000rpm or so in the case of most 6-Series. That full load programme must be five times what we used to do in the sixties. Then there are similar full load trials for things such as the differential to pass over 500 hours and the part load tests, where we run a mixed programme for at least 1500 hours.

'Even then you cannot say this is the test work behind a BMW engine, for there are millions, yes I really mean *millions* of kilometres to cover in cars. Winter testing in Sweden and Finland, plus other European locations. Hot weather testing? It used always to be North Africa, but now we do more, much more in the USA. In Africa the authorities were difficult and it is actually cheaper for us to test in America.'

It is also highly relevant to BMW as a large market, part of Georg Ederer's responsibilities covering emission and fuel consumption, all vital subjects in an American context for a European engineer. Much of the department's time has been spent meeting American emission standards, but part of the manpower problem is that US-standards are not the same thing as complying with forthcoming European emission levels, or the differing standards imposed by smaller markets such as Japan and Australia.

In the American market BMW have had to supply different six cylinder derivatives, which we discussed with Herr Ederer first. The important point to recall is that all these sixes are SOHC chain drive descendants of the original 1968 six, rather than the belt-drive overhead cam later design which you find in machines such as 320/520i, 323i. The economical 2.7 litre Eta engine, found in 5-Series when this was written, and destined (probably as a $2\frac{1}{2}$ litre) for 3-Series in Japan, and USA, uses the belt drive for its overhead camshaft.

Initial six cylinder coupé emission work concentrated on the previous model to 6-Series. Between 1972 and 1974 BMW offered the 3.0 CS in American power trim. This had a low 8:1 compression ratio, the usual Solex carburettors and was rated at 170bhp SAE at 5800rpm with 185lb.ft. of torque, roughly the same output as could be expected from the carburated 2.8 litre engine in both coupé and early 528.

As discussed BMW dropped the old coupé for the American market because of roof legislation, but the 5-Series became relevant in the 6's life once more. Between 1975 and 1977 BMW offered the 3-litre engine

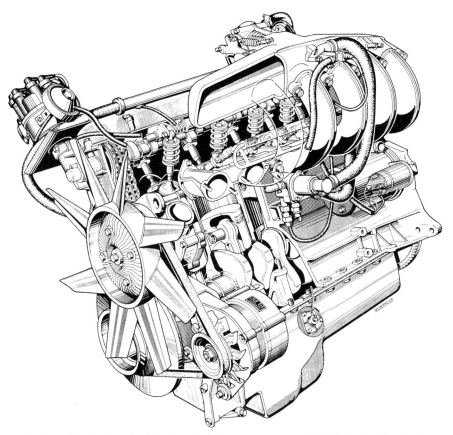

*The fuel injected unit of 633 CSi with generous sump, chain drive for the single
overhead camshaft and flat topped pistons clearly displayed, along with the distinctive
V-pattern valve gear angles from that single camshaft.*

within a device called 530i. This mated 2985cc with L-Jetronic fuel
injection from Bosch which Mr Ederer recalled 'because we have
changed over from D-Jetronic for this purpose and also provided a
thermal reactor, along with a low compression (8:1) and new engine
ignition timing to make it pass the emission regulations. This engine was
also used in the first American 630 model . . .'

Thereby hangs a tale. For 176bhp and 185lb.ft. of torque was not
enough to offset the weight of 6-Series in Federal form, some 3500lbs
leaving 0-60mph times way adrift of what was expected in this price
bracket and BMW's injected engine looking for US friends amongst the
critics, who usually plumped for Mercedes and Jaguar.

So BMW went back to the tough task of providing a cleaner exhaust and seductive performance in a package that measured the best part of five inches longer than its European counterparts and reflected that figure with a vehicle weight some 320lbs plus over its European cousin.

George Ederer recalled the result 'was a special version of the engine we used originally in 633i', with a three-way catalyst for the USA. Again BMW marketing logic suffered a slight spasm, for this 89×86mm version of the fabled six cylinder engine measures 3210cc and should have been badged 632 CSi, but the badge budget was all used up by that stage!

Once more the 3210cc motor used Bosch L-Jetronic fuel injection and the usual $30°$ slant installation, which did not harm the sweep of 6-Series bonnet line at all. This power unit has become the staple diet for big BMWs in the USA and can be found in 5, 6 and 7-Series. An absolute godsend to BMW has been the development of the Bosch Motronic engine management system with associated DME (Digital Motor Electronics) to handle the enormous variety of loads placed on a production engine in a country with such widely varying climatic conditions and altitudes.

Looking over the American model years you can see the power, torque and throttle response creeping back into the specification as the 3210cc was adapted with its Lambda sensor and three way catalyst to cope with life across the Atlantic ever more efficiently. For example the original 8.4cr of 1978 dipped to 8:1 and crept back to 8.8:1, close to the European level of 9:1 during the 1982-83 model years.

Similarly you could see power swarming back into the Bavarian six even for the USA. In Europe that 3210cc yielded 197bhp at 5500 revs with some 200lb.ft. torque. For the USA BMW began in the 1978 season with 177bhp at 5500rpm and 196lb.ft. of torque at 4000rpm. By the time 1982 models went on sale Robert Bosch's microprocessor electronics had helped provide American customers with 181bhp at 6000rpm and 195 lb.ft. of torque at the usual 4000rpm. The engine seemed happy to go for its 6400rpm redline and provided *Car & Driver* with 124mph, an EPA-estimated 19mpg and acceleration times of 7.7 seconds and 16 seconds respectively for the 0-60mph and standing $\frac{1}{4}$ mile sprints. That was in June 1983 and the price tag was $39,210, nearly double the figure American journalists had been complaining of for the original 630 CSi!

*A fine cutaway by BMW's usual, excellent artist, Niedermeier cross sections the
633 CSi and highlights the front mounted injection engine, capacious coil spring
suspension and four wheel ventilated disc brakes.*

European engine

George Ederer also conscientiously guided us through the development
sequence for Europe, where the big pre-production change was a last
minute abandonment of a 625. The 2.5 litre version of the previous
coupé was only made between 1974 and '75 as a direct result of the fuel
crisis and to show that BMW were not speed crazed by CSLs and the ill-
fated 2002 turbo street car. Originally the $2\frac{1}{2}$ litre's 150bhp and 156lb.ft.
of torque were scheduled for 6-Series, but even in the previous pillarless
coupé the weight had been 1400kg/3080lbs, and the idea of that $2\frac{1}{2}$ litre
powering an ostensibly sporting coupé that weighed at least 100lbs more
than its predecessor was finally enough to axe the project.

Coded E24 within the factory (E9 was the designation for the previous
coupé: E simply stands for *Entwicklung*, the German for development),
the 6-Series for Europe came in two initial engine sizes. They possessed
a bore and stroke size of 89×80mm for 2985cc with quadruple choke
Solex carburettor and the 89×80mm combination (for 3210cc) with the
L-Jetronic fuel injection. The carburettor fed 3-litre was a little more
powerful, with 185bhp at 5800rpm than it had been in the 3.0 CS (180 at
6000rpm); maximum torque was unchanged, but developed 200rpm
lower.

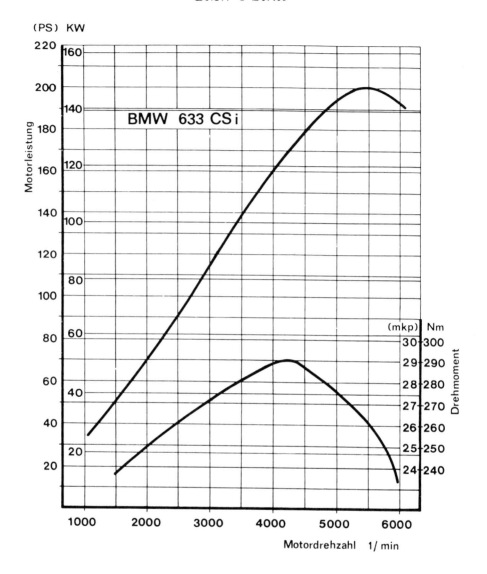

(PS) KW

BMW 633 CSi

Motorleistung

Motordrehzahl 1/ min

Power and torque curves for the carburated 630 CS and Bosch fuel injected 633 CSi power plants in 1976.

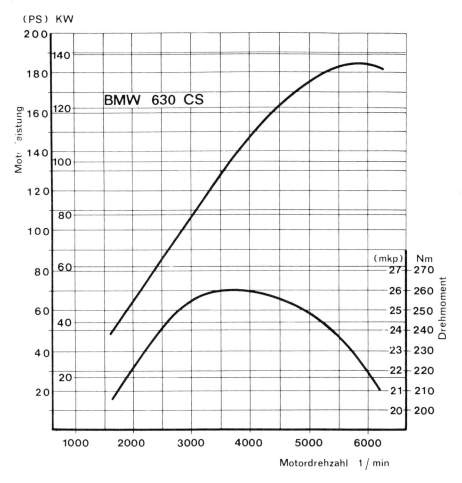

Why? Instead of twin Zenith 35/40 INAT downdraught carburettors BMW had selected the single Solex 4A1 design. In Ederer's opinion, 'this Solex design was from the American V8s and was usually called Quadrajet. It was an excellent carburettor with a big advantage in progressive power over the twin Zeniths; it was also easier to adjust and delivered an excellently controlled fuel/air mixture – but to service and manufacture this carburettor was a big problem for us.

'Over the years we did much work on good mixture distribution with carburettors. Always you seem to get liquid fuel delivered for some cylinders! So I am glad carburettors have gone on the BMW six cylinders. Now it is all taken care of automatically. Bosch receive engines and cars from us and do much development work of their own, but we also meet twice a week on average and we always have a large number of Bosch engineers working here as well.

'We were not the first to fit electronic injection from Bosch, but they had the idea for us to try the Motronic system first. I think it is because they were used to working with us and the department was small enough and dynamic enough to work with this new system. Fortunately it gave

Front view of an injected 1979 BMW big six emphasises the V-disposition of the rocker-activated valve gear beneath that overhead camshaft, and the hemispherical combustion chamber above those large pistons. The traditional slant installation angle is also revealed – particularly beneficial to the coupé stylists – and the simple, curvaceous tracts provided for ingress of air/fuel mixture, with similarly straightforward exhaust porting are also obvious.

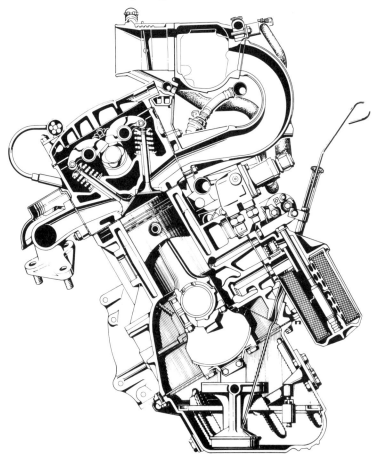

us no problems at all in service. In fact it gets rid of many service troubles...' It was July 1979 before BMW engineers were able to reveal this step forward, initially for the L-Jetronic equipped 3210cc motor of the 732i and 633 CSi, so we will detail the Bosch system with its 256-point timing memory in the appropriate chapter. Meanwhile a little more of another 6-Series that did not even make the February 1976 pre-production plan that the new E24 in 2.5 litre guise arrived at, only to be dropped before the April 1976 announcement of 630 CS/633 CSi. What about a turbo 6-Series counterpart to the 745i?

The good Georg shuffled his papers a little restlessly at this crass question. After all the 635 was an add-on to the original programme. BMW really had been serious about producing a less overtly sporting coupé for the eighties. So a 745i coupé equivalent was a much later consideration, for that 256bhp version of the faithful 3210cc did not appear in the saloon until July 1979 either.

Side view of the 1968 carburated six cylinder provided in 2500 and 2800 saloons/coupés of the period, although the 2.5 litre was not actually used in the coupé until 1974/5. The engine was basically a two cylinder bonus over the fours but detail work on crankshaft balance of the seven bearing unit, including 12 counterbalance weights allowed unbelievable smoothness.

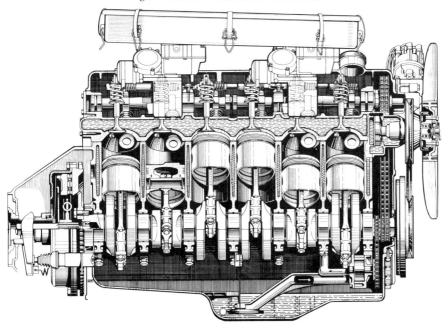

'Certainly this turbo was considered and we examined the coupé carefully with this possibility in mind. We did some paperwork in the seventies on this subject, but the big question was 'where to put the intercooler?' There simply was not the space in the engine bay that you can find in the 7-series. This would have been very expensive to solve, and we did not carry on with the project.' A big grin in conclusion from Georg Ederer.

It was time for us to clatter off down another flight of stairs in the austere office block that houses engineers who provided Europe's first ever production turbo, and who had a V12 within a CSL for production prototype analysis in 1972-73 ... We went away to ponder the 1984 rumours that BMW would be back with the V12 once again. For production this time, leaving us wondering whether it would appear in the 6-Series, or the long-rumoured mid-eighties successor that will share with the 7-Series the job of implanting a new and advanced BMW family look for the aero age.

From 4-WD in alliance with the 24 valve six, to the likely compact 12 that would result from paired M60 (the smaller six) motors, my fevered imagination wrestled with the permutations BMW may have to bring to bear if they are not to be squeezed from proud independence by Mercedes presence in the 190 versus 3-Series sector, to Mercedes' incredibly successful S-class. Or by pressure from Audi's resurgence on a Progress Through Technology theme, one that has already introduced a wider public to such features as 4-WD in alliance with turbocharging and wind-cheating shapes.

It's tough in the German upper classes!

Chapter Four

'A Legitimate Successor'

The key words above were spoken at the introduction of the new large BMW coupé 630 CS/633 CSi in Spain and accurately highlighted the problem of following such illustrious predecessors . . .

'For the joy of driving . . .' The lady gets to grips with BMW's latest driving machine in 1976, the fuel injected 633 CSi. Let's Go . . .!

March 1976: BMW are ready to publicise their new coupé thinking in Marbella, Spain and with the round of European motor shows, particularly the annual Springtime ritual of Geneva. To put the BMW launch into the perspective of the times, the fuel crisis is a fading two year old memory, with BMW making particularly good forward financial progress. The 1976 BMW four wheelers range from the 75bhp 1502, the last vestige of the 02 line hanging on in the wake of economy conscious motoring, to the 3.3 L, long wheelbase version of BMW's biggest pre-7-Series saloon. Between the 02 and those now old-fashioned large saloons, the BMW range makes more logical sense with earlier versions of the models we have today: the 3-Series then ran from the four cylinder 316 with 90bhp to the 320i with 125 horsepower. Next up were the 5-Series, which covered a 90bhp 1.8 litre four cylinder unit to a carburated six cylinder 528 with 165bhp. The saloon range then comprised, until the 1977 introduction of 7-Series, BMW's 2500, 3.0 S and 3.0 Si with L for Lang (long) derivatives with an extra 3.9 inches in the wheelbase and a choice of 2.8, 3.0 or 3.3 litre fuel injected sixes.

British customers waited only until October 1976 to receive the 6-

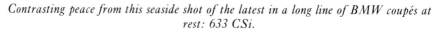

Contrasting peace from this seaside shot of the latest in a long line of BMW coupés at rest: 633 CSi.

Series, but the UK took only the 633 CSi injection model for the first two years, and the carburated 630 CS was never officially imported. In UK terms the BMW line of the time began with the £3118 1502, the 3-Series starting at £3849 in 1976 whilst a 528 represented £7679. Most expensive British market BMW of the period was the £13,795 long wheelbase 3.3 Lia, but the 633 CSi changed all that, priced from £14,799 in Autumn 1976.

Bernhard Osswald had retired when the public announcement of the 6-Series was made, his successor Dr Karlheinz Radermacher taking over as 'member of the managing board of the Bayerische Motoren Werke AG for development'. Herr Osswald was on hand to answer questions and Radermacher–who would be responsible for top level BMW engineering decisions until his abrupt 1983 departure in the wake of controversy over 3-Series quality, and the conservative way in which both 5-Series and 3-Series were revised for the eighties – paid positive tribute to Bernhard Osswald's development team work. Dr. Radermacher said, 'I wish to point out that it was my predecessor under whose direction this car was conceived, developed and perfected'.

Dr Radermacher went on to include the following remarks in an eight-page presentation. 'The lot of a successor is not an easy one, especially when the predecessor was a particularly successful type... So, in developing the new coupé our sights had to be set correspondingly high. It had to be a legitimate successor.' As when the 3-Series replaced the sporty 02 two doors, BMW were rightly concerned that some sectors of the press and public would not take to the more civilised, heavier, comforts of the newcomers compared with the legendary sporting success of its predecessors.

Judging from the heading in May 1976 MOTOR SPORT 'Munich Masterpiece' over an introductory story by Clive Richardson of generally warm tone, BMW need not have worried, but with the benefit of hindsight it is possible to see that the company may have underestimated the sporting aspirations of their customers, typified by the 1978 debut of 635 CSi and the M-power derivative of 1983 that emphasised this pattern.

The original specification
At the heart of any decision to buy a coupé rather than a saloon must be

an appreciation of the styling. Paul Bracq and the small BMW team had completed a body that drew admiration even from engineers within BMW, a body of men more impressed by practical performance than classic elegance.

One senior engineer told me that obtaining all round visibility whilst complying with the tough crash testing procedure with extra thick roof pillars had proved the major development headache on the body, but the time spent juggling the driving position inside the cabin proved worthwhile. The weight penalty, one which was always cited by BMW Motorsport as a prime reason for ignoring the new coupé in the early years, did not seem punitive (considering the extra sheet metal that had been crash test proven) according to the engineering figures.

Comparing the 6-Series (E24) with the previous E9-coded coupés BMW engineering cited 1450kg for the 630 CS and 1470kg for 633 CSi compared to 1400kg for the carburated E9 and 1420kg for the injected 3-

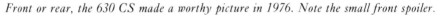

Front or rear, the 630 CS made a worthy picture in 1976. Note the small front spoiler.

litre 3.0 CSi equivalent predecessor to the 633 CSi. However, you could
see BMW Motorsport's point when you looked at the column containing
the CSL's weight, for engineering had that at 1165kg (rather than the
heavier public figures quoted in the previous chapter), providing a first
class basis for sport that had no 6-Series launch equivalent.

For comparison BMW engineering also highlighted weights for the
Mercedes 280/350/450 SLC coupés (1550 to 1630kg) and from 1120 to
1195kg for the Porsche 911 designs of the period, which even then included the Turbo, then a 260 horsepower 150mph 3-litre. Talking to
Bernd Quinzler, responsible for international BMW advertising in 1984, I
found that BMW strategy had been pitched very much as a halfway
house between the Porsche's sportiness and Mercedes' quality/
civilisation. Naturally it was BMW's contention that their customers
would receive the best of both worlds in the new 6-Series package . . .

Although it was built on that 2626mm/103.3inch 5-Series wheelbase,

Front or rear, the 630 CS made a worthy picture in 1976. Note the twin pipe exhausts.

The 630 at the Spanish launch: over 2,000 a year were built in the first two years, but the carburated coupé did not see the eighties.

the 6-Series used considerable front and rear overhangs to build the prestige link, and overall length, to a strong suggestion of 7-Series size. Thus it measured 4755mm/187.2inches compared with 4620mm/181.9inches for the 5-Series and 4860mm/191.3inches for the 2795mm/110inch wheelbase 7-Series. The width was closer to the 5 at 1725mm/67.9inches for the new coupé (some 25mm – or fractionally under an inch, more than for 5-Series) with a fashionable low look supported by a measurement of 1365mm/53.7inches for the first 6-Series and 1415mm/55.7inches for the boxy four door saloons in 5-Series. A 7-Series saloon is taller still, so BMW stylists had successfully produced a lowline coupé cousin with strong family identity and logic.

Today there is a lot more concern over aerodynamic efficiency than in 1976. BMW did not have their own wind tunnel until the eighties and it showed in some of the independent wind tunnel tests performed on the range a decade later, with figures well above 0.40, the company norm until the eighties facelifts. Indeed some models in the BMW range rated

The 6-Series making its grand entrance in Spain, March 1976. Even eight years later the basic lines were unaltered, but wider wheels and deeper spoilers have made their mark.

at over 0.45 Cd before 3-Series was facelifted in 1982.

At the time BMW said: 'tests conducted in wind tunnels have shown that the bodywork of the BMW 630 CS makes this car the most aerodynamic of all standard BMW models produced until today. The

Another from the Spanish album at launch time, exhibiting the original alloy wheel fitment and LHD market's preference for a single chrome mirror on the driver's side only.

small front spoiler underneath the bumper has quite a considerable influence on this good aerodynamic behaviour, and thus on the outstanding directional stability, resistance to wind from the side, roadholding and economy of the new coupé. In fact, the new coupé is 21 per cent better than the BMW 3.0 CSi in counteracting the upward pull of winds from beneath the car.'

There would be changes that improved both downforce and Cd figures for 6-Series, but in this original specification BMW laid the body story on a foundation of crash safety, all round visibility and cockpit layout with reference, as for the external style, back to that 1972 Turbo design study as a source of inspiration. Compared with the pillarless predecessor, 6-Series exhibited a quoted 69 per cent extra torsional (twisting) strength and an extra 23 per cent bonus in sheet metal 'crush zone'. You may curse the extra weight in the name of performance, but when an immovable object fills the windscreen outlook with inevitable crash speed, crush zones suddenly become welcome and relevant . . .

The cabin comfort was, and remains, exceptional. BMW's headline story was the test-branded array of seven green lights that hopefully illuminated on depression of the Test button. 'Hopefully,' because that indicated that all was well with: engine oil level; brake fluid; brake lights; cooling water level; screen washer level; rear (ie tail) lights and brake pad thickness. This Test board idea has since been widely used in the BMW range, usually working without the driver having to press a button these days and the basic principles can also be found in many of the fashionable digital dashboards from other manufacturers.

In the orignal 630 CS/633 CSi you can see the basis of the eighties' models, with a deliberate creation of the wrap-around cockpit feel to the cabin. In LHD for 1976 you would grasp a sturdy four spoke steering wheel amidst an interior notable for the wide use of BMW-developed and manufactured plastics. The horn buttons were inlaid into each steering wheel spoke. Ahead under that single viewing pane were three large dials: combined fuel and water temperature gauges; a 240km/h

The 1976 test unit on the LHD model shows the seven checks that could be performed on press button command: oil level in the engine; brake fluid; rear brake lights; engine cooling water level; windscreen washer water; rear lights operational and brake pad condition.

The LHD and British RHD dashboards photographed to show their 1976–79 layout with the most pronounced 'cockpit' feel seen on a BMW up to that point. The high grade fascias are made and assembled by a Bavarian BMW subsidiary factory, arriving at Dingolfing plant, ready to install.

speedometer with separate total and trip distance recorders, plus a 7000rpm tachometer redlined from 6500 onward.

Steering column levers controlled the traditional quick-action functions such as flashing indicators, headlamp flasher and windscreen washers, just as they do today. The central fascia sweep carried some switchgear – notably the small pushbutton that illuminated when the rear screen heater elements were activated, and the heater/ventilation controls. These included the variable fan speed control, capable of fooling any stranger, being operated via the clock's bezel ring. Electric windows, where fitted, were commanded from switches either side of the gear lever. The latter would control a four speed manual transmission, the Getrag 262/9 with Borg Warner synchromesh components, or the three ratio ZF HP-22 automatic transmission with Fichtel and Sachs torque convertor. Both 630/633 shared these gearboxes and a 3.45 final drive ratio was standard for 630 CS, with 3.25 for 633 CSi. In general BMW transmissions, more particularly the availability of myriad options, are a complex subject and one on which an author is unwise to be inflexible in saying that a particular year must have a particular specification!

Originally it was hoped that UK 6-Series CSi models would come with a limited slip differential set at 25 per cent locking as standard. That did not happen for these initial coupés, but as with the fitment of a five speed gearbox in later cars – which could have closer sports ratios or the overdrive fifth and wider intermediates – you may well find a coupé in which the owner did specify an LSD. In America the 1982 model year 633 CSi was specified with a five speed gearbox as standard, but the ratios were not the same as for the European 635s.

The 1976 630/633 models had four speeds with the following gear ratios: first, 3.85; second, 2.203; third, 1.402; fourth, direct 1:1. These were exactly as for the previous coupés, which also used either 3.25 or 3.45 final drives. The ZF automatic offered planetary gear variations based on: first, 2.478; second, 1.478 and a 1:1 third and final ratio. All the manual models used a single dry plate clutch (MF 240) of hydraulic operation.

Compared with the previous pillarless coupés, the new BMW's body advantages were not confined to the extra strength of the integral rollover hoop within the centre B-post pillar. Luggage capacity was up

Boot space was generous by the standards of most coupés, with the emphasis on lengthwise loads, rather than depth. As ever the toolkit is a useful masterpiece in itself.

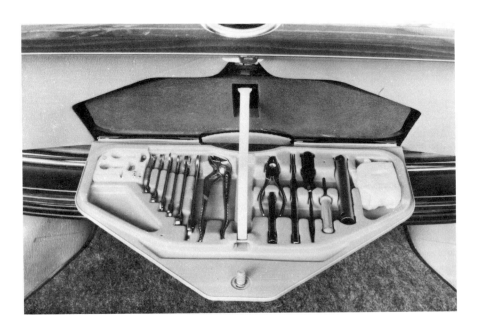

by 23 per cent to 14.6 cubic feet instead of 11.8 cubic feet. In practice this means two Brits can buy crates of duty free French booze, add it to the personal debris and luggage accumulated in a week's travel across Belgium, Germany and France, and still close boot lid via the push button without rupturing its hinges!

The accent on creature comfort, compared with earlier BMW two door coupés, was apparent in the use of 91lbs of sound insulating material instead of 50lbs. Similarly glass area was up, somewhat surprising in view of the need for extra pillars on 6-Series. BMW said the increase was 7 per cent. A bit more important to those in sunny climes was that Parsol Bronze heat resistant glass was standard, whereas it had been a special equipment item on the 1968-75 coupés.

Seating was sharply improved and included provision for driver's seat ride height adjustment in the basic 6-Series specification. Confirming the comfort attack heater output was boosted from 6500kcal to 8000, up 23 per cent, but more important was that the previous BMW weakness in flowing air through a cabin with extensive glass area (coupé and 02 series) was plugged with plenty of adjustable fascia outlets and a 31 per cent increase in air flowed through said cabin. For the USA in particular the air conditioning was asked to provide extra refrigerating capacity: 6200kcal instead of 4500.

The alternator remained rated at the 770 watts of late model 3.0 CS/CSi coupés, but battery capacity went from 55 amp/hr to 66, all on a 12 volt system of course.

Engine moves

Underlining the work put in by Georg Ederer and his colleagues, outlined in the previous chapter's interview, was a long list of specific changes made to the inline sixes for the new coupé. The carburated 630 CS and the injected 633 CSi were notable by today's standards in selecting a common 9:1cr instead of the 9.5:1 that had been available in the 3.0 CSi. Eighties coupés have reverted to the trend for increasing, rather than reducing, compression ratios in the quest of efficient combustion.

As always the sixes used triple hemisphere combustion chambers within that 9:1cr layout in alloy, a design feature that promotes a

Neat rear headrest touch was the inclusion of this small storage compartment, often used to put emergency medical supplies within.

swirling action within the combustion chambers. Such principles are basic to BMW's belief in maintaining a good proportion of European power in countries with stricter emission laws, and originally allowed them to live on the American market with rather less emission control equipment than most rivals.

How fuel was delivered to serve in the combustion process showed continued progress. Georg Ederer commented on the four choke Solex carburation fitted to 630 CS in our interview and this was the reason for an extra 5bhp quoted 200rpm lower than for 3.0 CS, bringing the 1976 coupé total to 185bhp at 5800rpm. The peak torque figure remained unaltered at 188lb.ft. but here the new coupé had to go to 3500rpm instead of 2700.

For the injected models, a Bosch L-Jetronic system meant the more sensitive detection of airflow rates within the fuel injection unit via a

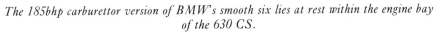

The 185bhp carburettor version of BMW's smooth six lies at rest within the engine bay of the 630 CS.

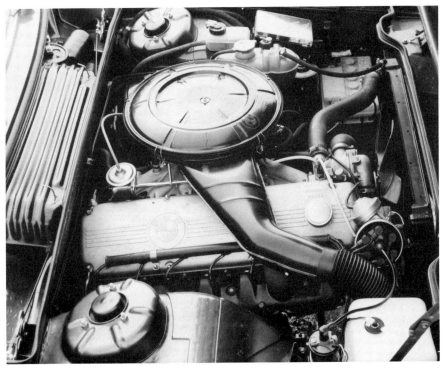

One for the badge freaks and collectors. This is how it was in the beginning . . .

meter to govern fuel proportions, whilst the previous D-Jetronic apparatus relied on partial vacuum measurement inside the intake manifold. The 3210cc engine in 633 CSi thus developed the same 200bhp at 5500rpm as its higher compression 3-litre cousin, but the extra cubic capacity also brought 210lb.ft. of torque at the power peak instead of 200lb. within 50rpm of the previous figure. These 3.2 litre European figures were given at the launch: in 1984 the equivalent 3210cc quotes were 197bhp at 5500 revs and 209.5lb.ft. at 4300rpm, listed only for 732i.

Engine cooling was given greater attention in the 6-Series with a Holset-coupled viscous fan of 16.5 in girth, up nearly an inch over previous six cylinder practice, but the big change for the better around the engine was in the use of breakerless transistorised ignition for the 633. The 630 CS stayed with coil and contact breaker systems and their attendant increased maintenance demands.

Steering a new course

Those who had owned examples of the 1968-75 BMW coupé range probably noticed most driving change immediately they operated the steering at anything much above parking speeds. ZF ball and nut hydraulic power steering with a 14.5 steering box ratio (16.9 overall replaced the 18:1 overall ratio used between 1968 and 1975), but far more importantly the power assistance from the servo system was set to provide *less* assistance at speed. This transformed the driver feel of the power-assisted car, for as you went faster the steering became heavier, just as though it were a manual arrangement. Such power assistance is now commonplace, but only thanks to the efforts of BMW and Mercedes who ensured that the roads of Europe didn't have to be tackled in the traditional one-finger power steered manner popularised in American cars – or their GM/Ford/Chrysler cousins overseas.

Even today the steering input to a driver's palms is markedly different between those traditional rivals Jaguar, BMW and Mercedes, the British car favouring an extremely light action, made a little heavier with the deletion of one tooth from the rack, but still transatlantic in the effort required at the rim. That the Jaguar rack and pinion is precision personified is in no doubt, but there is also a strong suspicion that drivers who buy machinery such as the 6-Series prefer to feel what is going on, particularly on the side of a frozen Alp!

As implied by our interview with Walter Stork a great deal of general chassis work went on to make the 6-Series a far better choice than one might have expected from the retention of the usual MacPherson strut

The new BMW coupé was not such a sporting machine as its immediate CSL and CSi predecessors, the accent on elegance and creature comforts initially. Handling was typically BMW with this kind of understeer quickly converted to a tailslide under full power on those comparatively narrow wheels and tyres.

front and trailing arm back end that is the BMW tradition. However, before becoming too warm about how much better the 6 was than its predecessors, it is relevant to note that the old coupés were nothing special in the handling department. Good fun, but not particularly efficient at restraining the inevitable waywardness of 200 horsepower applied to a wet city street, one that had been lovingly finished in a slick of truck diesel to provide the kind of coefficient of friction skid schools adore.

The handling point was that the 1968-75 BMW coupés were continual updates of what had originally been a conversion from the early sixties BMW four doors with four cylinder power. The legacy was a narrow rear track: 1402mm/55.2inches instead of the front's 1446mm/56.9inches. That fundamental point was tackled with a wider rear than front end on the 6-Series: 1422mm/55.9inches leading a 1487mm/58.5inches at the back end on the later purpose-built BMW coupé.

After that the handling was fine tuned with reduced caster angles and increased kingpin inclination, plus the use of a rear anti-roll bar that had not been generally available throughout the previous range. At the front, anti-roll bar diameter increased to 24mm rather than the old coupé's 23mm, getting closer to a full one inch thickness, whilst the new rear bar was of a 16mm/0.63inch circumference. Camber angles were left the same at the front, very slightly positive: $0° \ 30'$, a full degree more inclination than had been exhibited on the earlier coupé. Again this led to more chance of rear end grip under duress, but with negative camber angles the designer's problem is that a consistently heavily laden car will tend to wear the inside tread of its tyres at a high rate, the inside doing more work under low cornering or heavy luggage loads with a negative camber layout. Negative camber is identified from the rear by the disposition of the wheel and tyre, apparently splayed outward at the lower edge, often with the outside of the tyre tread clear of tarmac until the machine is actually cornering hard.

The comfortable character BMW had aimed at with 6-Series was generally reflected by increased suspension travel figures, up to 4.5 inches at the rear end. The overall effect with the 633CSi was of a car less prone to follow bumpy road cambers, one that was appreciably more comfortable to travel in over said bumps, but generally less sporting in

Driving position can be adjusted fore and aft, up and down; backrest angle (note slide knob for rear access) — and the steering wheel is also adjustable for distance and angle. They defy you to be uncomfortable! In the back there's the same standard of trim with those neatly retracted rear belts between the seats, but space is at a premium, in line with the 2-door coupé image.

character, although the speed-sensitive steering drew favourable comment to compensate.

Braking? As discussed, dimensionally the units had a lot in common with 5-Series, but were ventilated all round, rather than just at the front, as on 528/528i. For BMW in coupé terms the major step forward was in uprating the old coupé's 272mm/10.7inch ventilated discs into 280mm/11.0inch fronts whilst retaining the same vented rear 10.7inch layout. The caliper specification of the front discs remained the same through the size multiplication, but a pad wear safety warning was part of the 6-Series check system. Servo unit was a Mastervac 9 inch unit on the new 6-Series.

Before we leave the 1976 specification and explore what sort of performance was provided, note that a wide variety of options particularly on the less extensively equipped German market machines were offered right from the start. The January 1976-printed catalogue that I was given in Munich shows that an alert owner could have specified Recaro seating, three spoke sports steering wheel of 380mm/15inch diameter, a 65amp alternator, leather trim and a complete sports suspension pack, including 'tilt angle stops on the front spring struts, modified front stabiliser bar, reinforced rear stabiliser bar, sports-tuned springs/shock absorbers.' What you could get varied according to the market concerned. For instance the standard wheel and tyre combination was an alloy 6J × 14 H2 unit with 195/70 VR radials, frequently by Michelin in British examples. An American 633 CSi started life with 7J BBS-Mahle alloy wheels, whereas the original US-market 630 CSi offering had the usual alloys and visually different rear end bumper treatment.

As ever, there were a lot more extras, from air conditioning to headlamp washers, that might be part of the basic specification in countries used to paying more for their BMWs, typically Britain. The determined BMW enthusiast could find any number of specialists keen to fit individually tailored equipment, factory-made or otherwise. So you might well find an oddity such as a five speed gearbox or a $3\frac{1}{2}$ litre engine with front and rear spoilers amongst these original 6-Series, but BMW did not make it that way to begin life in the fast lane! Mmmm, unless you have struck very lucky indeed and found a car tailored by BMW Motorsport for their own use, or that of contracted drivers...

Performance

Although the whole launch philosophy was built around distinguished coupé heritage and style, rather than rampant performance, no 6-Series deserves to be labelled as anything other than rapid transportation for road use. There was not an immediate performance successor to the legendary CSL in the new BMW range, but what they had was enough to attract customers adman Bernd Quinzler described as being typically, 'above average intelligence. They may not see motorsports, but they are interested – and they have the personal qualities of a competitor, wanting to beat others. They do not like to show off: we have a slogan that we used that sums it up, "Our status is not on the hood (meaning the marque badge – J.W.), it's underneath." Our target group is one that likes understatement and that is one of the reasons people call us conservative in our body styles . . . or worse!' Herr Quinzler concluded.

In the table you will find the km/h figures and UK/USA equivalents provided by BMW at the press launch for 6-Series performance.

630 Cs	All times, seconds	633 CSi
0-50km/h (31mph)	2.7	2.6
0-80km/h (50mph)	5.9	5.6
100km/h (62mph)	8.9	7.9
0-120km/h (75mph)	12.4	11.4
0-160km/h (99mph)	23.4	20.9
0-400 metres ($\frac{1}{4}$ mile)	16.3	15.8
Maximum, mph	130.4	133.5

In general these figures were realistic predictions of production performance, but American customers will remember that their 630 CSi had a hard time braking the 0-60mph ten second barrier and the 1978 model year onward 633 CSi in Federal trim was over half a second slower from rest to the mile-a-minute mark than its European counterpart. Top speeds would have been around 122 and 125mph respectively for those two US-bound coupés.

Fuel consumption? Hitching up an automatic to the six did hurt mpg badly in British conditions. One of the major BMW dealers reported, 'London users can get down to a regular 14-15mpg with an early auto and 17mpg is not uncommon out here in the country. The newer models are *much*, much better.' For a four speed manual 17-19mpg seemed usual, these figures for fuel injected 633 CSi and likely to represent better overall consumption than 630 CS managed.

Independent UK tests by *Autocar* and *Motor* generally showed better mpg than anticipated above and at least the performance BMW predicted, if not more. *Motor* managed 134mph maximum against *Autocar*'s 131 and *Motor* also held the 0-60mph upper hand with 7.8 seconds reported against *Autocar*'s 8.1 seconds. Both magazines returned closer to 21mpg overall. In US terms those represent around 25.2mpg and I can almost hear the hollow laughter across the Atlantic, the probability for emission models was beneath 20mpg in their original guise. The 1983 EPA Estimated figure for 633 CSi was 19mpg.

American performance levels for the 1983 model 633 CSi are pretty respectable with 7.7 seconds reported 0-60mph and a 16 second standing quarter mile from *Car & Driver* in June '83, coupled to a two-way average of 124mph. Over $10,000 less and slightly quicker (127mph; 15.8s $\frac{1}{4}$ mile) was the 533i four door, but when the customer wants a coupé, he wants a coupé really badly!

Did the customers take to the new coupés in 1976? Not without BMW making some swift changes . . .

Our hero 633 gazes out to see what's at sea . . . It should have foreseen the longest production run of any 6-Series derivative.

Chapter Five

Evolution, Not Revolution

Karmann initially constructed the 6-Series, just as they had been responsible for earlier BMW coupés, and they manufactured 2072 of the 630 CS in that first 1976 sales season that followed the car's public debut in March at the Geneva show. As ever in BMW coupé tradition, the more powerful and larger-engined variants tended to do better and Karmann made 2862 of the injected model in 1976. If you look through 6-Series coupé production figures since the start the 635 CSi was the only model, up until the close of 1983, to exceed 4000 units a year. So we are talking about a comparatively rare mass production model, as well as seeing that BMW's customers tend to go for the fastest and best-equipped derivatives in the coupé line.

However, all was not well at the start of the latest BMW coupé's career. The Americans were not overjoyed at the performance of their ex-530i fuel injection version of 630 and BMW were seriously concerned at quality complaints that they felt rested with the coachbuilders. Neither were press and public overawed by the performance of 630 CS and 633 CSi. As ever there were some sharp comparisons with beloved BMW predecessors on the sporty side, for there was no CSL excitement allowed at this early stage in the new coupé's career.

BMW acted on the quality front to bring as much of the assembly job 'in-house' as fast as possible, also changing the American recipe with alacrity. From August 1977 Karmann were confined to making metal, delivering a steel bodyshell in primer by road to the sprawling and continually expanding buildings beneath huge chimneys at Dingolfing. Today, the arrangement continues, using road transport for a production rate that needs road transport flexibility to match a demand that peaks in Summer at possibly 55 coupés a day and slumps to 30, or

91

A somewhat stony road had to be surmounted before the present production standards could be reached . . .

less in the winter seasons. For BMW perspective you need to know that Dingolfing serves to top up 3-Series production, making about 250 a day in addition to the 550 or so that they can make in Munich. On the same lines as the occasional 6-Series, Dingolfing's 14,100 workers average about 500 of the 5-Series saloons and about 200 of the range-leading Sevens. So the 6-Series coupés are very much the low production centre

Inside the Dingolfing plant the bare 6-Series starting point as it arrives from Karmann.

of attention. However it is only fair to say that, in May 1984, myself and a colleague visiting Dingolfing were most impressed with the hard work and paintwork preparation/finish that goes into *every* BMW.

The employees, particularly those who have to fit up sub-assemblies to the engine/gearbox/front suspension package that is offered up beneath the car, earn every Dm they get. For they have to keep precisely on the pace of a line that makes little fewer cars than some Ford Escort production plants – and do it with a finesse to satisfy a far more fickle public. Besides which there are 800 quality control personnel to satisfy, 30 checkpoints to pass and a separate department that pays individual attention to coupés, with slightly different $1\frac{1}{2}$ hour road tests for *every* M635 imposed. Soon each coupé is likely to receive similar treatment instead of the present varying percentage, although all have ten minutes operational check on a rolling road.

Back in 1977 BMW were concerned that the trim fitment and water leak problems were eliminated from the early 6-Series, and high pressure water tests continue to be part of the build and checking process today. In 1977 BMW also had to find some more power for the clientele and the Americans got priority (would I suggest they hollered

93

The main assembly halls at Dingolfing where fast workers demonstrate their versatility on the 5-, 6- and 7-Series that pass along the same lines. Each to his own exhaust . . .!

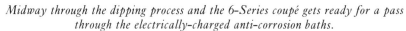

Midway through the dipping process and the 6-Series coupé gets ready for a pass through the electrically-charged anti-corrosion baths.

loudest? Surely not, with an American contract making this book possible . . .) from the 1978 model year.

The answer was the Federal 633 CSi based on the 3210cc six cylinder engine that was, and is, shared for North American BMW use by the 7 and 5-Series four door sedans. It had little more horsepower than the injected 3-litre that preceded it, but far better driving manners. A useful torque bonus won the 633 CSi a place in the market more worthy of the 1981 American catalogue description for 633 CSi: 'A high performance coupé, as opposed to a high performance facade.' By then an 8.8:1 compression ratio had allowed 181 SAE horsepower and 195 lb.ft. of torque to restore increasing respectability to BMW's North American coupé performance. These 1978 model year 633 CSi coupés also had the wider Mahle wheels and new rear bumper treatment to differentiate them from the original Federal 630 CSi.

In Europe performance was a priority too. In July 1978 the Bavarian Motor Works presented the model which was to become the most numerically popular in production in the eighties and said, 'introducing the 635 CSi, BMW is launching the fastest four seat coupé made in Germany—a new model designated to supplement the 630 CS and 633 CSi series.' In fact the 630 CS stayed on for just another year and the 633 CSi's sales task became a deviation to America and other lands where its emission certified six was vital, although markets such as Britain took the 633 as an automatic until 1980.

As ever at BMW the essential excitement of the newcomer lay in the engine. This 93.4×84mm (3543cc) SOHC six was, and is, credited to BMW Motorsport development, because the cylinder block marked a rather daring oversize bore that Paul Rosche had originally been told was impossible when he had wanted extra capacity for the 'Batmobile' CSL coupés of 1973. To credit that relationship the 635 CSi six was coded M90, and its cylinder block descent from the M49 racing engines of the seventies and the M88-coded four valve per cylinder unit within the mid-engine M1 was also duly publicised.

As introduced in the Summer of '78 there was no faulting BMW's logic, for the 3.5 litre provided 218bhp with 5200rpm civility. Plus a torque curve that looked as though one could build a decent apartment block on it, using that broad spread of more than 191lb.ft. provided between 2000 and 5900rpm, as foundations! The maximum torque

Three steps to motorised heaven. A six cylinder engine trundles along the track to join a Federal 633 CSi. Note the size of the gearbox, attachment of propshaft and full suspension/ventilated disc brake assembly that has already taken place, before the power train is offered from beneath the coupé.

report of 224lb.ft. at 4000rpm was almost a by-product in comparison . . .

The 635 motor was the first of the 6-Series to follow the eighties bias toward high compression ratios, rated at 9.3:1. Detail installation changes that complimented the fitment of the bigger bore, shorter stroke engine, included ensuring that the fuel/air metering of the Bosch L-Jetronic fuel injection was updated. Exhaust gases could be more swiftly removed too, for the exhaust pipe diameter went up from 633 CSi's 42mm/1.65inches to as near as dammit a sturdy two inch bore (1.97inches for pedants).

The MF 240 diaphragm spring clutch had its pressure plate springs strengthened and a five speed Getrag 265/5.70 gearbox was standard equipment. The introductory ratios centred on a direct top and a raised 3.07:1 final drive in place of 633's 3.25 and the earlier model's 3.45. A ZF limited slip differential was frequently fitted, but remained clearly on the option list in major markets. For example in 1984 the UK were offered the limited slip as standard on manual 635s and a £322 option with automatic.

Now with 140mph pace and a conservative 0-62mph acceleration claim of 7.3 seconds (most of the UK independents got 7 seconds or less for 0-60mph) Walter Stork's suspension men started specifying

Der neue BMW 635 CSi.
Es gibt Ideen, die zu gut dafür sind, nur einmal eingesetzt zu werden.

Deshalb hat BMW das 3,5 l Rennsport-Triebwerk nicht nur als Grundlage für die drei Motorversionen des M 1 benutzt, sondern auch als Basis für das 160 DIN kW (218 PS) Triebwerk des neuen BMW 635 CSi.

BMW 635 CSi: Neue Kraft für eine erfolgreiche Idee.

Ausgehend von diesem neuen Triebwerk bieten wir mit dem BMW 635 CSi ambitionierten Fahrern ein neues Konzept: die Mitte zwischen der komfortablen Sportlichkeit einer BMW Limousine und dem sportlichen Extrem des BMW M 1. In der zeitlos eleganten,

unaufdringlich sportlichen Form des BMW Coupés führt ein neues System von Leistungssteigerung, Drehmomentverbesserung, Fahrwerks-Modifikation und aerodynamischen Hilfen zu Fahreigenschaften und zu einem Fahrverhalten, mit dem der neue BMW 635 CSi ehvr an Wettbewerbs-Fahrzeuge als an Serien-Automobile erinnert.

BMW 635 CSi: Extrem hohe aktive Sicherheit durch ein neues Fahrverhalten.

– Verstärkte Stabilisatoren an Vorder- und Hinterachse.
– Zusätzliche Wankneigungsanschläge an den vorderen Federbeinen kontrolliertes Ausfedern, erhöhte Wirkungsweise des Stabilisators. Begrenzung erhöhter Karosserieneigung im Kurvengrenzbereich.
– Straffere, doch komfortable Feder-/Dämpferabstimmung.

Bei der Auslegung des 5-Gang-Getriebes wurde insbesondere Gewicht auf den Geschwindigkeitsbereich zwischen 100 und 180 km/h gelegt. Gerade hier entwickelt die BMW 635 CSi ein faszinierendes Beschleunigungsvermögen: 0–100 km/h 7,5 s, 0–120 km/h 10,1 s, 0–160 km/h 18,3 s. Höchstgeschwindigkeit 222 km/h.

noch besserer Fahrbahnkontakt unter allen Bedingungen.
– Breitere, 6,7 Zoll Leichtmetall-Felgen, größere Aufstandfläche, bessere Seitenführung.

Die Leistungsfähigkeit des Fahrwerks wird durch aerodynamische Maßnahmen optimiert. Das Ergebnis: im Mittel 15% weniger Auftrieb vorn und hinten, noch bessere Kraftübertragung auf die Fahrbahn, noch höhere Kurvengeschwindigkeiten und bessere Fahrzeugstabilität und damit eine Verschiebung der Grenzbereiche nach oben.

Die BMW Coupés:
630 CS, 633 CSi, 635 CSi
Kauf oder Leasing – für beides ist Ihr BMW Händler der richtige Partner.

BMW – Freude am Fahren

The 1978 BMW 635 CSi is introduced to the German public via press advertising stressing the engine's links (based on the same 3.5 litre iron cylinder block) as the mid-engine M1 lurking in the cargo bay above its spoilered flanks. In Germany the range continued to offer 630 CS and 633 CSi as well.

Unusual threequarter top shot shows the additional front and rear spoiler area to advantage in the 1978 BMW 635 CSi.

Contrast: in the Summertime 635 racing driver Hans Stuck completes another photocall for BMW Munich, whilst the winter picture shows the conditions that so often greet the high performance car tester in Bavaria!

subtle suspension modifications. Front spring travel remained the same, but at the rear the movement was stiffened and restricted with heavy duty roll bars also specified front and back. 'Anti-tilt blocks' to limit roll were also introduced to the front strut springs.

Most obvious chassis change was to the wheel equipment, 6.5inch 'spider's web' BBS Mahle light alloy types replacing the usual 6inch alloy. Tyre size remained at 195/70 VR on the previous 14inch diameter.

The 11inch front discs and 10.7inch rears were left alone, but a comprehensive glassfibre front spoiler in matching body colour and a deformable plastic bootlid air dam modified the aerodynamics as well as adding sales potential! BMW said, they reduce uplift by an average of 15 per cent. This greatly improves directional stability at high speeds', and I certainly would not quarrel with that statement, although the firmer suspension added a great deal of driver feel and confidence in the

The original equipment for 635 was this BBS styled and Mahle cast alloy 6.5in. wide × 14in. diameter wheel. This one is wearing the standard 195/70 Michelin and also exhibits the practical body side rubbers that do much to take the sting out of supermarket parking tiffs.

The RHD 635s started arriving in the UK later in 1978, but this is an example I was allowed to borrow in late 1979. Then the price had risen by £700.

The extended front spoiler and thick rubber rear air dam are beautifully portrayed in the shot of M1-owner Dirk Strassl at play in the 1978 BMW 635 CSi. The aerodynamic drag factor of the sporty BMW coupé was improved, but the bigger bonus was in all round stability at speed.

The 1978 back spoiler was a more solid affair than today's rear spoiler, and carried the BMW badge. The motif is now back in the bootlid in the current coupés, as illustrated by this 1983 Group A racing 635 at Donington in the author's track-testing hands.

new coupé recipe from BMW.

Britain got the 635 CSi with RHD at a theoretical snippet of under £16,500 and continued to receive the 633 CSi, but only in CSia three speed automatic specification at £15,379. I say 'theoretical' in relation to 635's October 1978 launch cost, for a heavy armour plating of extra and supplementary charges is a feature of RHD models. By June 1979 *Motor Sport* could report a basic cost of £17,199 and extras adding another £2132!

If you are buying secondhand it is as well to know that air conditioning originally cost over £1000 extra in the UK and a sunshine roof demanded more than £550, so fully-equipped cars represent better value overall. Note that from April 1980 RHD 635's had headlamp wash-wipe, heated door mirrors, passenger seat height/tilt mechanism and the option of that sports direct top gear five speeder, or the overdriven ratios (as specified as standard US equipment in the eighties

The extended BMW 6-Series coupé range at rest (at a guess at the quiet Murnau hotel frequently used by the company to assist new product launches), with the 635 on the left, 635 also centre, arranged to show off the BBS Mahle wheels and interior, with a 630 C reminding us of the original shape and alloy wheels.

catalogues I hold) as part of the standard specification; the gearbox alternative being a no extra cost option.

By then BMW had made some major 6-Series changes. These were announced for the German market in July 1979 and rode on the back of a heavily revised 7-Series. Major 6-Series addition was at the start of the range, now all fuel-injected. For the sweet 2.8 litre familiar from 528i was inserted with its 184bhp. Its normal and sturdy dimensions of 86×80mm (for 2788cc) were equipped with the same 9.3:1cr as 635 premiered and was reckoned to provide about 130mph. The car was not overburdened with standard equipment, looking almost old fashioned without the usual spoiler 'beard' of 635 and many contemporary cars and it weighed 70kg/154lbs. less than the orignal 635. As a result acceleration was still not far off that of the four door saloon, which weighed over 200lbs. less again, at some 9.0 seconds from rest to 60mph. Effectively this model replaced the carburated 630 C, which ceased production in July 1979 with just 5763 made, only 249 of them in that final production year.

The 633 CSi equated to the 7-Series 732i in Europe, both using the 3210cc engine that has the Federal emission counterpart, but rated at 197hp on 5500rpm and 210lb.ft. of torque at 4300 rpm in European guise, both falling into line with this Summer '79 update in the use of a 9.3:1cr too.

This 3210cc engine was also the first, and for a while the only, BMW six with the Digital Motor Electronics (DME) mated to the Bosch L-Jetronic injected engine. Engine ancillary changes covered a new dual pipe exhaust unit with larger intermediate silencers and a wide use of stainless steel. Certainly the comprehensive silencers and wide use of stainless steel are effective. The exhaust systems are an imposing sight at Dingolfing—as are the debit digits in your bank account, when it eventually does come up for replacement!

Weight reduction was tackled in 6 and 7-Series by more efficient utilisation of the sheet metal needed in safety crumple zones and non-load bearing areas of the unitary steel bodies. However there was also a dietary aid in the form of an aluminium radiator which, BMW claimed was, 'not only lighter, but also more efficient in cooling'.

All BMW six cylinder engines used transistorised ignition without contact breakers, but micro-electronics brought new possibilities to precise control of vital ignition and fuel feed functions. At the heart of the DME system is a mini-computer programmed to activate correct ignition timing, fuel and air mixture settings, the precise moment to inject fuel under widely differing circumstances (from Alaskan cold start to Mojave desert work out) and to take into account varying barometric pressures and outside air temperature in making such calculations. Using an ignition performance graph with load points and engine rpm BMW say '256 memory locations are obtained. Each of these memory locations can be filled with an individual ignition time. Due to the enormous speed of computation, at every revolution a new calculation and sensing can take place, so that optimal ignition timing is always maintained.'

With such micro-electronics there is nothing to wear out and the valves do not need to be service maintained, as was the case for the original contact breaker ignition systems, or is the case for mechanical

The 3.5 litre engine for 635 in 1978 was formally rated at 217.5bhp by BMW, enough to provide 138mph, a very similar performance to that of the 206bhp CSL from the previous series. In 1982 the six was replaced by a slightly smaller bore 3.4 litre.

BMW overseas press manager Michael Schimpke is closest amongst the Dingolfing onlookers as the virtually complete six heads for another quality check, hoping for a BMW badge, at the last check out ceremony.

components. However, programming the brain is a time consuming and expensive business, as many racing teams have found out both in Formula 1 (where BMW also use Bosch computer-processed engine management, and have done since the start of their turbo GP engine programme) and in saloon car racing, where one of the first priorities on 635 was to 'brainwash' the management system in its new high power, high fuel consumption role . . .

Electronics expertise also extended to the option of a complex on-board computer for the post-July 1979 big BMWs with 12 basic functions, red LED readouts, and a vehicle anti-theft code that has been known to lock out senior BMW personnel on first acquaintance. The computer is useful but making it a servant rather than an arrogant, chiming, taskmaster has led to a later, simpler, generation of BMW cockpit computers that surfaced with the new 3-Series in October 1982.

In 7-Series saloons July 1979 was a truly significant date, for the turbocharged 745i was also introduced at this point and a completely new 'Doppelgelenk' (double linkage) front suspension debuted to 'allow steering offset to be laid out over a widely variable range'. At the rear an anti-dive linkage was provided and both these features eventually found their way onto the 6-Series, but not the new 7-Series interior. Instead owners of the coupés were reminded of progress by the installation of an LED digital clock, in place of the analogue companion of the earlier seventies.

These 1979 changes did not happen all at once to the 628, 633 and 635 CSi coupé range, but wherever components were the same as on 7, the appropriate common change was made. Incidentally it should be noted that the 7-Series saloons, even in the 137mph turbo 745i trim, were not allowed the coupé's vented rear discs. Furthermore the diagrams for front suspension clearly show the second link suspension for 7s and not

In July 1979 BMW could advertise on the home market that the time had come for the exclusive coupé class to embrace a new generation, the 628 CSi, whose time had come. The sweet 2.8 litre, ex 5 and 7-Series, was the least powerful engine fitted to the coupé.
Yet its 184bhp still provided 130mph pace and BMW pushed the advantages of electronically-minded injection on this model and digital motor electronics (covering the ignition as well) for the 633 and 635 CSi models that completed the home range, the 630 C effectively superseded at this point.

107

The 628 CSi on the driveway outside BMW's United Kingdom HQ, arriving at just under £17,000 in October 1980.

for the coupés at introduction time, for the coupé had to wait beyond June 1981, when 5-Series adopted the suspension changes, before they could be adapted to 6-Series.

The 628 CSi arrived in Britain with RHD and a price tag of just under £17,000 in October 1980. At this stage it was also noticeable that some minor detailing work had gone on for the 635, with a slightly shallower back spoiler outline, standard velour trims and central locking that could be controlled from the boot, or the passenger door. More importantly the 3.5 litre engine gained the Digital Motor Electronic system of the 3210cc pioneers. The 633 CSi was still available in the UK with automatic ZF transmission at £17,462 but this was the last year in Britain for the 633, leaving the choice of 628 and 635 CSi models that still prevailed in 1984.

Hans Erdmann Schonbeck, BMW sales director, and original Flying Finn Rauno Aaltonen spoke persuasively in Munich of the next step in the coupé's progress. The grey-haired Schonbeck, resplendent in an immaculate blue blazer, told us at a presentation held in part of the BMW executive canteen on that hot international press presentation day; 'welcome to the totally revised BMW 6-Series, the second generation of the BMW coupés first introduced in 1976. Approximately 35,000 vehicles of this series have rolled off the assembly lines, so far, a high figure for this class of automobiles.'

Externally there was little sign of the considerable mechanical and weight-saving change that had been made. Just a new front apron and closed bottom to the engine compartment betrayed that BMW were becoming more concerned with aerodynamics, whilst the rear bumper was extended to provide better protection at the sides. Standard wheel sizes became 6.5 J × 14inch with 205/70 VR tyres on their alloy rims, but British 635s and those for many major markets will be more familiar on the multi-spoke and odd-sized alloy rims that support Michelin TRX 220/50 VR 390 (15.35inch diameter) low profile and steel-braced rubber. Those with really sharp eyes could peer at the headlamps and note a stepped reflector dividing the lamp with a lower half to provide better side and short distance 'fill-in' illumination. Fog lamps were integrated with the front end panelwork (which followed the Seven in offering a generally softer, flowing, interpretation of the original Bracq Turbo-inspired shape) and at the rear, high intensity fog warning lights became production items too.

By 1982 the 635 had been modified in a number of fundamental respects, but the principles of injected six cylinder power and trailing arm rear suspension remained. Performance was a little better thanks to a consistent diet and subtle aerodynamic changes dropping the two door down to 0.39 Cd.

Additional link

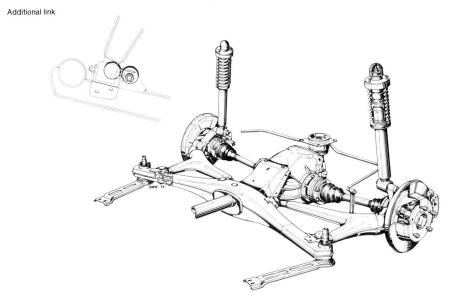

The 1982 BMW 6-Series picked up the 528i's use of the 13° rear trailing arm layout and additional top mounted link. Note that the 1982 cars have quietly dropped the use of ventilated rear disc brakes, falling into line with 5-Series too.

Internally the weight reduction progress was a spectacular average of 60kg/132lbs. as the body could now be further lightened in line with the later steel technology and the knowledge of crash test standards prevailing, rather than those anticipated at the design stages. A kerb weight of 1430kg was given for both models, contrasting with 1500kg originally claimed for 635 and 1450kg for 628 CSi.

The chassis was totally overhauled. BMW engineers had been forced to wait for some 7-Series components, like the full double link front suspension with reduced steering roller radius, and the similarly 5-Series debutant of 1981, a relocated trailing arm angle of 13° and its articulated overhead linkage placed behind the axle line. Since the 5-Series had adopted such features in 1981 – although the re-mounted trailing arms were initially confined to performance derivatives such as 528i – it was logical that the coupé should also benefit from a layout designed to cope with bumps, puddles and tyre deflations with minimum front end drama. Plus a rear layout that tidied up the BMW's manners in a tail-slide, and also made such excess throttle skids unlikely on a dry road with the broader TRX 50 per cent aspect ratio tyres

110

installed. Net result? A far more roadworthy car with far less reaction to sudden bursts on the throttle, or sharp decelerations.

'New' engine

In the Summer 1982 modifications the 635 truly became a 634 and it emerged that BMW had suffered a service problem with the previous Motorsport-inspired 3453cc engine and its 93.4mm bore. So they reworked the faithful slant six into yet another permutation, allying a 92mm bore with the 3210cc's stroke of 86mm to produce the present European 6 and 7-Series 3½ litre power unit used beneath 635/735 badges. It actually measures 3430cc and power is quoted as the same 218bhp at 5200rpm with an unchanged torque peak.

Engine detail work for the 3.4 litre newcomer comprised an increase

The front suspension is also substantially different from the original layout, although variable ratio power steering remains as trustworthy as ever. Note the double link strut principles of 7-Series have been adopted, then adapted via 5-Series for BMW's prestige coupé.

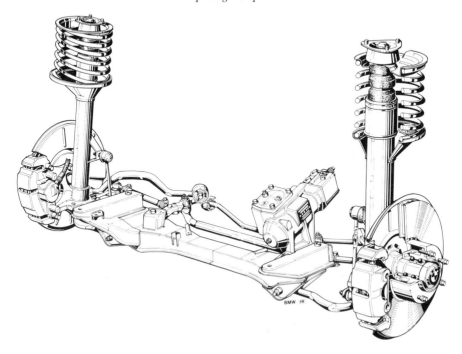

BMW 635 CSi
Sonderausstattung:
Metallic-Lackierung

Inside or out, the new Motronic II equipped 3.4 litre of 1982 onward is a significantly different engine to the original 3.5 litre, although both were rated at 218bhp. Injection manifolding with centre 'box' section provides fastest visual identification of the newer power unit for 635.

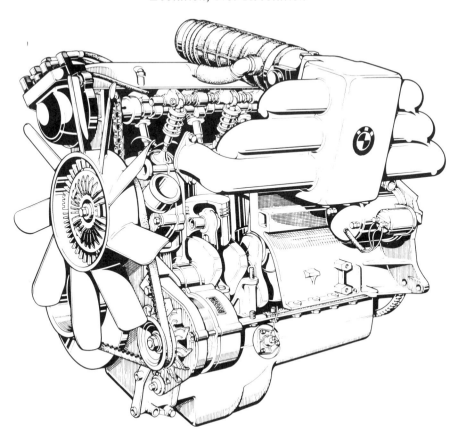

in compression from 9.3:1 to 10:1 and utilisation of the second stage in Digital Motor Electronics (which added a fuel mixture graph to that of the ignition) that was augmented, via another graph specifically to control the warm-up cold start phase, in the search for improved fuel consumption. Idling speed was knocked back 50rpm and the fuel shut-off point on over-run was shifted to 1000rpm. The later 3430cc engine was mated as standard with an overdrive five speed gearbox to achieve 13-15 per cent quoted consumption savings along with lowered weight and the reduction of idling speed – which may not have sounded much at 50rpm, but of which BMW said; 'nearly two thirds of this success are thanks to the reduced idling speed'.

The new Sixes were very promptly phased into the RHD schedule and are credited with arriving in the UK in June 1982, complete with

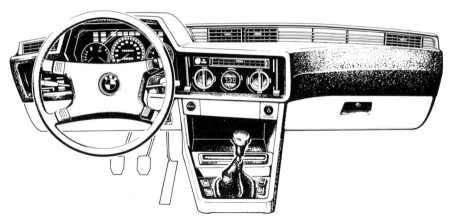

The changing fascia of 6-Series is depicted in drawings of the four spoke steering wheel 1979 model (with a digital clock in the centre console replacing the first analogue fitment) and the three spoke steering wheel of the current mid-eighties layout, introduced in the Summer of 1982. The latest dash includes Service Interval Indicator and an mpg/litre per 100kms. monitor in a layout that continues the cockpit theme, but varies considerably from the original. Note that the test button centre of 1976 has stood the test of time (left of steering wheel).

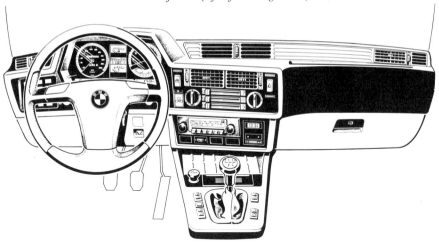

ABS anti-lock braking, on-board computer, the service interval indicator and a modified interior that featured three spoke steering wheel and a three lever, thermostatically operated heating and ventilation system. The now LCD readout of the digital clock was lower down the fascia and the instrumentation behind the traditional single pane was considerably altered. The same speed, rpm, water temperature

Current 628 CSi in RHD form with TRX wheels and a price tag little beneath the £20,000 mark, reveals very slightly softened nose contours of 1982 onward.

and fuel contents were monitored by dials, but the style was new and the speedo incorporated a fuel economy indicator that was electrically connected, rather than the notoriously inaccurate vacuum manifold 'econometers' beloved of mass manufacturers.

UK introductory prices were £17,895 and £22,950: writing some two years later the tags read £19,275 for 628 and £24,995 for big brother. So it's always best to get on and purchase a BMW as soon as finance allows, rather than waiting around for the virtually unknown price drop or discount special. Even at that price for 635 it is worth noting that air conditioning is a £1374 option and there are plenty of others to allow customers' price totals beyond £26,000 very rapidly . . .

Performance of these 'second generation' 6-Series was much as before but fuel consumption could be substantially changed by the transmission specification. In Britain today the 635 is sold with no extra cost alternatives of ZF's latest 'switchable' four speed automatic gearbox, or the standard OD five speeder, or the quintuplet, direct top, close ratio cluster. On the manual transmission front that means BMW quoted an average of 26.6mpg for the OD five speed-equipped car, 24.5mpg with the sportier gear set, or 24.45mpg in automatic transmission trim. Today that latter figure could be further modified by quoting the figures in the Sport or Economy modes of the ZF automatic box, but I think we've got enough figures to baffle everyone without resorting to pedantic dirty tricks . . .

More everyday relevance can be obtained from *Motor*'s overall 22.5mpg for a manual 635 of July 1982 which had managed an observed 137.1mph and 0-60 in a fine 6.9 seconds. The same weekly British magazine also tried the 628 CSi, but in 1980, and reported 0-60mph in 8.3 seconds and 19.8mpg overall. *Autocar's* figures were available to fit later and reported 139mph, 0-60mph in 7.3 seconds and an average 21.8mpg. Like the author they had not experienced a 628 CSi as at the close of 1983. Incidentally UK availability of automatic transmissions included arrival of the four speed unit with its immensely tall top gear in January 1983, and the switchable unit a year later.

Production rates did increase for the European line of 628/635 and the

Detailing in the current 632 automatic shows the three optional modes available to the drives from the auto selector; the production rear spoiler of 1984 and the TRX wheel and tyre offering that was standard on a 15.35 inch diameter rim in UK (Opposite).

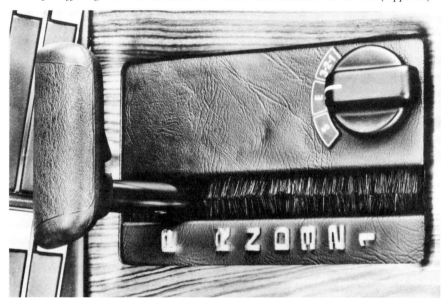

BMW 6-Series

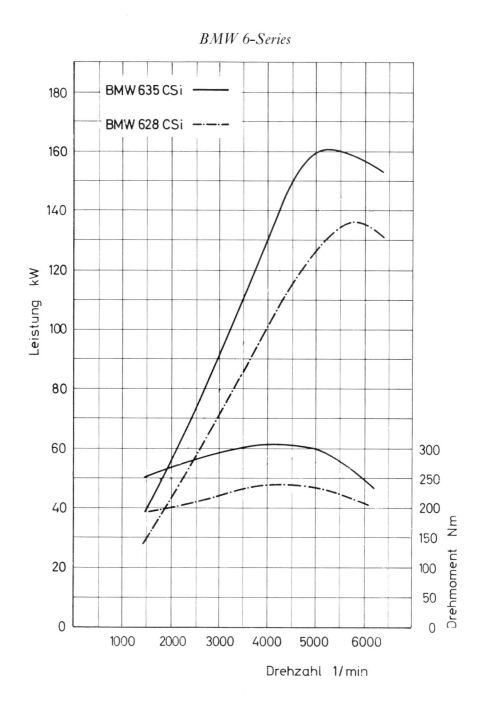

Graphic illustration of 628 and current 635 engine performance on the test bed.

Heavily equipped RHD 635 CSi leaves little change from £25,000 and shows how the auxiliary lamps were neatly faired into the revised front spoiler of 3.4 litre models.

mainly US-bound 633 CSi has also fared better in the recent eighties, although another 62 units in 1983 would have been needed to match 633 CSi's peak in serving all main markets with 3387 copies during 1978. The 635 proved the big seller, as well as giving BMW Motorsport an incidental basis on which to support saloon car racing with a current coupé, after seasons of backing the obsolete Karmann coupé of 1968-75 outline–and CSL specifications.

In its first year the 635 sold 1286 and the following 1979 season brought 3775 sales. That was a record exceeded in 1982 with the aid of the new model (4153) and nearly matched for 1983 with some 3673 sold. This compared with 3324 of 633 CSi and only 972 of 628 in the same year, a total of 7970 BMW 6-Series manufactured in 1983. In 1982 they made an overall 7601, well up on the depressed 5652 of 1981, a lower figure for 6-Series production than at any time since 1978's meagre 5597.

'Number crunching' a little further (a process aided by Richard Feast of *Automotive News* and the German Verband Der Automobilindustrie; VDA), we find that individual total coupé production to the close of 1983 stacks up as follows. Champion with 21,889 examples produced

New York hustler: the 633 has served the coupé cause well for BMW North America.

from 1976 to 1983, and the only survivor of the original range, is the 633 CSi. Then with two seasons fewer in production, and no USA market, came the 635 with 19,087 produced. A year younger, but definitely the collector's choice on rarity value, must be 628 CSi with 4173 made: even the 1979-buried 630 CS managed 5763.

Taking all models for a final grossing-up we find BMW had made 50,912 between 1976-83, handsomely putting to rest the 44,254 final figure for the preceding 1968-75 BMW coupé series. So the move to 6-Series sophistication was commercially justified in numbers, but only once the sporting 635 had lent some 140mph muscle to the argument.

Now let's look at the beefiest production BMW 6-Series to date: M635i.

Chapter Six

A Six with New Heart

'The M635 CSi is many things all rolled into one without being a compromise: an elegant, classical coupé combined with an intriguing extra margin of performance and pure driving pleasure.' That is how BMW in Munich saw the M-coupé when sales had begun in Spring 1984. Then the price was 89,500 Dm, equivalent to £23,995 on the home

If you wonder what the word oversteer means, this gentleman at BMW's Ismaning test track demonstrates. A classic BMW handling illustration, showing the ultimate roadgoing statement of BMW's 6-Series: M635 CSi.

market. Sales were expected to reach beyond the 1000 mark, instead of the originally planned 400-off, but there was no way that the M for Motorsport badge looked likely to be used to redress 1984's increasing domination of the European Touring Car Championship by Jaguar. BMW officials reiterated patiently that there was no way that engine manufacturing inside the Munich plant could cope with making 5000 of these 24-valve M635 power plants in a year, although prominent BMW 6-Series competitors such as Hans Stuck had originally hoped that the engine would be used to ease the power deficit of racing 3.4 litres against Jaguar's superb 5.3 litre V12.

When we visited Dingolfing in Spring 1984, just before the IG Metall strike started bringing Germany's motor industry to an unaccustomed seven week halt, along with most other major European motor

Nelson Piquet, Brazilian ambassador for jokes in GP racing, the 1983 World Champion. Nelson claimed that title with a 1½ litre Brabham BMW turbo four cylinder product of BMW Motorsport origin, and poses with the BMW Motorsport developed M635. At Hockenheim in August 1984 he picked up an all black version, with enlarged (3.7 litre) six producing 330bhp and capable of over 170mph!

manufacturers dependent on vital components such as those from Robert Bosch and Mahle pistons, we could see that output of the M635 CSi was truly integrated with normal BMW output. Then the M-coupés were trickling along at about two a day, or about 500 a year. An extraordinarily thorough road test and series of quality checks marking it out over the already thorough progress checks made not only on 6-Series but also on the other BMW models that you can also see steaming along the same overhead tracks. British supplies of the M635 were scheduled for January 1985 when this was written and BMW GB (Bracknell) Product Manager Chris Willows told us what was expected. 'Before the full effect of the strike could be judged we hoped for January 1985 for M635, and the factory have always assured us that supplies would be in RHD. Standard equipment will obviously be to the kind of fuller specification that we prefer in the UK. You cannot be talking of a car that will be any less than £30,000 with the on-cost of RHD, and items like the wider wheels and tyres that are German options, all in the UK price.' As in Germany the pricing of Porsche's 310bhp 928S seems to be a guideline, and that was over £32,200 in Britain when we talked to BMW at Bracknell, who expected 'between 100 and 120,' of the M635 to sell in 1985. No sales plans in the USA were mentioned at any stage, but the States will presumably be one of the priority targets when a rebodied coupé is launched later in the eighties . . .

MPower

From a T-shirt to the side of Nelson Piquet's World Championship Brabham, the MPower legend is conscientiously promoted by BMW, and the coupé expression of that philosophy is six inline cylinders with double overhead camshafts and 24 valves to provide an independently timed 150mph, 0-60mph acceleration in $6\frac{1}{2}$ seconds and a standing quarter mile in 15.1 seconds with a terminal speed of 95.7mph. In other words a 6-Series that Moves with a capital M, whilst still providing 19mpg in the hands of *Performance Car*, the UK monthly magazine that provided those typical fifth wheel independent test figures. However there were plenty of testers who got a longer run at measuring maximum speed and came closer to 155 of the 158mph claimed by BMW.

Although BMW Motorsport also uprated every other component

needed to compliment such stirring performance – brakes, suspension, transmission and interior – the key to this character is that magnificent motor.

We went along and talked to Georg Thiele at BMW Motorsport's Preussenstrasse headquarters, perhaps the most presentable sports emporium the writer has seen in 17 years nosing around, or working within, major manufacturer's competition departments. There is a large showroom to the street front, displaying everything from complete cars to delectable leather jackets, but behind lurks a quadrangle of assembly workshops and test cells that make BMW Motorsport a miniaturised version of the parent company. It is not just a one floor deal either. Below you tend to find the tentacles of Paul Rosche's engine empire with safe-like steel doors and testing equipment that can run any engine up to GP power level through a complete race track simulation, or a simple airflow cylinder head test, as required. Above the ground floor are offices of all kinds, housing heavier and heavier engineering talent to the back of the quadrangle and the administrations around, and including, Rennleiter (race leader) Dieter Stappert, above the street front.

Georg Thiele (left) explains his M635 development of the M1 engine to the author at BMW Motorsport in Munich. Note individual throttle butterflies and carefully crafted linkage for the six injection inlet tracts.

BMW stressed the link between 6-Series and M1 once more, but this time over 90 per cent of the basic engine made the trip from the middle of M1 to the front of 635.

In pursuit of M635 knowledge, we interviewed the man responsible for the practicalities of an engine programme that was initiated in 1980. Georg Thiele had a lot of existing knowledge to draw on in developing the $3\frac{1}{2}$ litre six a stage further: competition with the older coupé, and inside the M1 mid-engined machines, and street use of the M1. Yet there were some important advances in driving manners and fuel economy that engine management systems would make possible, and there was the need to install the motor at the traditional BMW saloon car slant of 30°, rather than vertically, as in M1. Installing the six cylinder car's individual exhaust pipes at the critically correct lengths took up much of that development time . . .

First there was the basic starting point of a 3453cc BMW six (93.4mm bore × 84mm stroke), dimensions that came from Motorsport originally and that served on the road and track for M1 and the 635 CSi before the Summer 1982 reduction to 3.4 litres (92 × 86mm). That meant items like the basic 635/M1 bottom end, with an immensely tough forged steel crankshaft, were in the specification from the start. However, note that the M1 employed race-style dry sump lubrication, *not* the usual roadgoing wet sump system that M635 employs.

'Fuel economy and good town driving manners were very important in our development programme' reported Herr Thiele with a gentle smile, bravely struggling with the unfamiliar use of English, or my patchy German, as he outlined the detail work that turned the 277bhp of M1 into a more refined 286 horsepower for M635. The later car also developing 250lb.ft. of torque at 4500rpm instead of M1's 244lb.ft. at a more peaky 5000 revs.

The principles are the same as when Paul Rosche and the team turned the four valve per cylinder six from the earlier coupé's racing power plant into a unit for the M1 that could be used on the street. 'Valve sizes

The original M88 racing 24 valve engine of 3½ litres was first used in the 1974 fuel crisis-curtailed racing programme for the previous BMW CSL coupé. By 1975 it was producing a regular 430bhp, but vertical installation brought it closer to 470bhp, the trim in which it was raced within BMW M1. Paul Rosche's road version of this powerplant became the 277bhp powerplant of the late seventies M1.

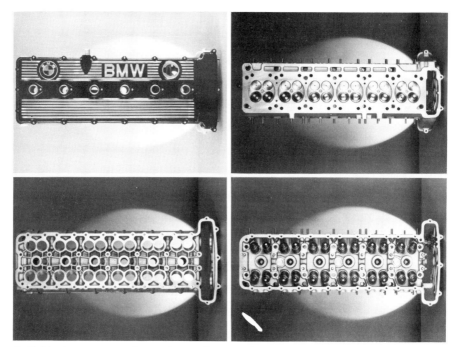

Individual components that go into making up the BMW DOHC, 24-valve power unit, including the black rocker cover with central plug hole access carrying two BMW badges, the four valve per cylinder combustion chamber with centre spark plug; bare head casting without the valves and their springs; plus a picture to show those items with their new adjustment caps.

are the same – 37mm inlet and 32mm exhaust – and the camshafts are of 264° duration that Rosche made for M1 – but we have made some important new parts. The cylinder head is the same casting, but with modifications to the water ways and inlet tracts to suit the 30° mounting. The waterways are no bigger than before, but they work with an inlet system that is re-angled to suit the slanted engine.

'The way in which we arrange the tappets is completely new. Instead of the cap underneath, where everything must be taken apart to make an adjustment, we now have the plate over the tappets, so you can make an adjustment by changing the plate, because the tappet now works directly. Also the adjustment for the air flow in the fuel injection system is with a balance pipe and a central screw, instead of the awkward screws we had on M1.' Indeed the single shaft and ball-jointed throttle linkage is a work of art in itself, as I hope you can see from my pictures, which

A comparatively long connecting rod and shorter piston than M1 used, complete with 4mm valve recess toward the outside edge of the piston crown. Oil ring control and number of rings has changed since the days of M1 too.

Another look at the aluminium cylinder head casting, which accommodates chain drive for the overhead camshafts and uses a new method of valve spring location to speed adjustment maintenance procedures.

should also show that they retained the individual throttle butterly system of the roadgoing M1, rather than the single guillotine slide preferred in racing.

Statistically the biggest cylinder head change shows up in the adoption of a fashionably high (10:5:1) compression in place of the M1's 9:1 but it's also relevant to note that the M635 gets much of its priority town manners and low fuel consumption from the use of Bosch ML-Jetronic injection and second generation Bosch Motronic engine managements. It may be unglamorous to work on the lowest possible city idling speeds for such a glorious power unit, but Motronic and that revised injection with its precise idling adjustment allowed Motorsport to match the close ratio-geared 635 CSi on official fuel consumption figures with remarkable improvements at certain points. The figures? At a constant 56mph you may find the M635 returns 36.2mpg (7.8

It may use a lot of ordinary mass production accessories these days, but the 24-valve, DOHC, engine is far from ordinary within!

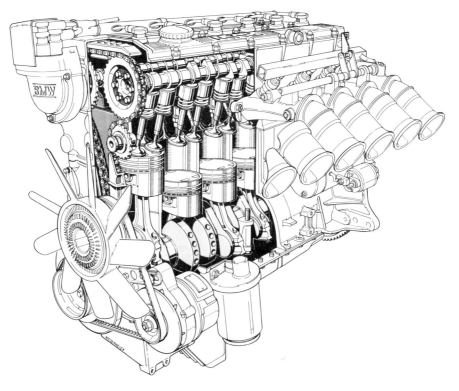

It took them years to make that exhaust system work efficiently within a slant installation, beneath the road M635 coupé's bonnet. On the 'cold side' we can see the electronic injection system that has done so much to benefit road fuel consumption and traffic manners. Note the large wet sump layout; the M1 and the racing models all used dry sump lubrication.

L/100kms) compared to the 12-valve coupé's 34.8mpg (8.1 L/100kms). At 75mph both are dead equal at 29.1mpg (9.7 L/100kms), whilst around town there are only fractions between the 24-valve engine capable of 286bhp and 12-valve engine rated at 218bhp: 17mpg (16.6 L/100kms) for the lower power engine and 17.1mpg (16.5 L/100kms) for the autobahn-stormer! In American terms that means the detail work on M635 has brought the Munich missile into a range from 20.5 City use mpg to 43.2 US mpg at 56mph, almost an econo car in performance motoring terms . . .

If you look at the graph Herr Thiele has on his wall, you can see that both 635 and its M-coded brother have much the same consumption up to 100mph, the Motorsport car drinking more heavily as it starts to work harder to ultimately greater speeds. This is a stark contrast to the 745i turbo saloon, which has an awful fuel thirst as soon as any boost is needed, and generally a rather more erratic fuel and power curve.

Although the basically 3-into-1 exhaust manifolding 'took practically the whole time to make right, with good power, economy and to fit in the car,' other engine ancillaries were simplified considerably, compared with its mid-engined forerunner. For example the wet sump uses the same pan and 6.5 litre capacity as a 218 horsepower 635. The oil and water pumps are the same as 635 and use the same belt system. The 80amp/1120 watt alternator, viscous fan coupling, starter motor and single crankshaft damper is the same as for the slower, series production 6-Series.

Georg Thiele pointed out, 'on the M1 it was necessary to have the double crankshaft damper for rpm over 7000. On this car there is a limiter for plus or minus ($\pm$) 100rpm at 6900. Also, we should say that the chain drive for the overhead camshafts is not the same as M1: that had a two-row Duplex chain, this one is a single row, smaller, chain drive.'

Whilst assistants gallantly carted in complex cylinder head castings, complete with superbly crafted injection systems and linkages, Georg continued his painstaking, but never boring, insight into the latest translation of MPower that was developed as M88/3. 'The pistons and connecting rods are completely new, with the 3.5 litre engine's steel crankshaft. The pistons have different oil control rings: the M1 had them above the connecting rod bolt hole and now they are below. This

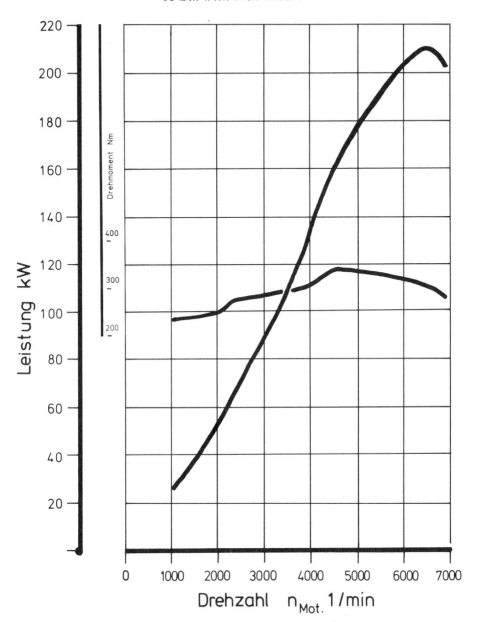

Power and torque curves for the 286bhp Munich motor within M635. It delivers much the same horsepower as the company's Group A racing 12-valve, SOHC, engines within the 635 CSi, but with traffic manners and respectable fuel consumption.

With the normal 635 alternator in the foreground, and its external head water passage creeping around the black case for the camshaft-driven distributor, the M635 power plant is the Dr. Jekyll and Mr. Hyde of motors.

goes with new piston crowns for the 10.5:1 compression, but also the cylinder bores have a special honing treatment. It is a special cross-hatch treatment for good oil consumption and lubrication control and high rpm. It is *not* on the 2 valve per cylinder engine of 635, just for this M-car.' A similar process is used upon the bores of the F1 unit.

You would think that this complex power house would extract a painful weight penalty, but Georg Thiele reported, 'just 15kg' more than the usual 635 motor, about 33lbs. So now it is over to the transmission and chassis men to discover what they did, aside from relocating the battery in the boot to counterbalance some of this front end weight bias . . .

Chassis finesse

Competition chassis engineer Werner Frohwein assisted by Herr Frings finished up with a 1500kg/3300lb. M-parcel to play with, carrying

Installed within the coupé, the 3453cc seem to fill every nook and cranny with the promise of power almost unlimited.

53 per cent over the front wheels and 47 per cent over the rear. Complete with the bodywork and running gear changes that we discuss later, the M635 was rated with a drag co-efficient of 0.39 Cd with 53.3 inch height, and track figures of 56.3 inches front and 57.6 inches rear with the standard wheels and tyres.

What it meant was a vehicle substantially the same as 635 CSi in dimensions, plus 70kg/154lbs. on catalogued weight and with the potential to reach at least another 10mph maximum, with acceleration rates that would need to be countered by better brakes and suspension.

Aided by the translation efforts of Peter Löcker, known to many of BMW's sporting customers, we discovered that the technical problems for Motorsport were really not the obstacle. Company senior management caution over any new derivative was far more of a restriction than any technicality, for BMW Motorsport had been building and experimenting with various four valve combinations since 1977, when they had tried the 24-valve motor in 5-Series. This merely

Uprated Bilstein-damped suspension is complimented by 300mm × 30mm thick disc brakes at the front, and Ate alloy brake calipers.

fitted in with their usual exploratory moves of engine and model combination, and no official work on the MPower 6-Series, outside the engine, was seriously undertaken before the eighties.

An M635 body is that of a Karmann-built 635 CSi, but they do have to massage the rear floorplan heavily to install the larger 7-Series final drive. Standard production wear inside that diff is a 25 per cent ZF locking action, as optionally available on cheaper Sixes. Other important transmission moves are related to a completely new bellhousing that is integral with a Getrag 280/5 gearbox of five speeds, arranged in the traditional competition pattern with first isolated and closest to an LHD pilot.

Gear ratios are new: first, 3.51; second, 2.08; third, 1.35; fourth a direct 1:1 and fifth an overdriven 0.81. The latter is asked to cooperate with a 3.73 final drive instead of 635's 3.07. Drive is still taken up by a large single dry clutch plate, but the springs are considerably stronger. Even with the usual hydraulic leverage applied, you need a suitably

Here the squared off front spoiler and extended arches are most noticeable, driver's wiper carrying a small aerofoil to complete the conversion!

sturdy left leg to control clutch action accurately and consistently. The revised gearing allows 159mph at the rpm limit of 6900.

The body has very slight flares to the wheelarches to accommodate standard 220/55 Michelin TRX on 165 TR 390 alloy wheels, or the optional BBS three-piece alloy wheels of 210 TR 415 dimension that accommodates radical 240/45 VR TRXs, the lowest and widest TRX ever to be fitted to a BMW. In inches it means that a 6.5 × 15.4inch cast alloy is replaced by the racy BBS of 8.3 × 16.3inches, the extra inch of diameter needed to compensate for that ultra low profile, as well as offering the best part of two inches extra rim width and an adhesive radial, nearly 9½inches wide. This is a *road* car!

The suspension sounds straightforward with the usual BMW MacPherson strut front and the now 13° angle of back trailing arms, but it is stunningly effective. Spring rates were stiffened 'some 15 per cent front and rear and about 10mm removed from the ride height. We used the Bilstein gas dampers specially developed for this car and also went up on the roll bar thickness. At the back we use a progressive bar that

Our test RHD 635 CSi pursues the M-coupé to highlight the minor style differences, such as the front spoiler and widest TRX optional wheels, outside the Munich office block.

gives an effect where only 0.5mm increase gives an effective strength like you had added 2mm,' recalled Herr Frings. He also added the information that a supplementary helper spring was installed within each front strut. 'This is to counter the body roll you would otherwise get at the cornering speeds this M-car can go,' he said with a small smile that spoke of treats to come, when we did get a chance to experience the most exhilarating BMW production 6-Series so far.

Brakes were naturally uprated, the emphasis being placed on front-end stopping power. Instead of 280mm by 25mm thick (11inches × 0.98inches) they installed 'new development' cross-ventilated discs that measured a hunky 300mm × 30mm (11.8inches × 1.18inches) with four piston matching calipers from Ate and the old M1-specification. The discs are also grooved at the front, but at the back the usual 272mm/10.7inch vented unit is fitted, but braked with pistons having an extra 2mm/.08inch circumference. The complete ABS anti-lock braking system had to be matched to the high

Interior improvements include these superb seats with a wide range of adjustment, and a chunky steering wheel to keep them company.

grip, weight and performance of the M635, for ABS is a standard equipment item.

Ancillary cooling work to the main engine installation comprised a 'larger and thicker' water radiator core and a thermostatically governed oil cooler. After all we are talking about an engine that develops the 218bhp of the usual 635 at only 4500rpm . . . A fabulous power unit in the BMW tradition that is likely to spend much of its hard working life delighting owners at 6000rpm, or more.

The M635 is the ultimate expression of the current 6-Series on the road. Now we see how Munich's reputation for fast track coupés was upheld by the 635 CSi in a Europe that was attacked with great vigour by the reborn Jaguar company. Those of great BMW loyalty should not read beyond 1983's fantastic final round where your favourite marque comes out on top. In 1984 things changed . . .

Capable of over 155mph and 0-62mph in 6.4 sec, the M635 does not get much of a chance to rest and show off its subtle alterations.

Chapter Seven

Racing 635: Some You Win . . .

Replacing the racing BMW 'Batmobile' CSL coupé with the 635 was a far more protracted business than had been the case in the showrooms of the World. It is nice for any manufacturer to have a model that is such a firm favourite that it goes on winning years after its production line death, but in BMW's case the CSL was so effective that the car was still winning four *years* after BMW had ceased production of the 1968-75 coupés! In 1979, the final season in a series it first won in 1973, and then dominated in terms of outright European Championship victories, the winged CSL won 12 of 13 qualifying rounds. It captured the title once again, and was only beaten by a BMW 530i in the round that got away!

Just as Porsche tended to dominate long distance sports car racing, whatever the rules, BMWs tend to be on top when the hours (anything up to 24 in qualifying rounds) of European saloon car racing are complete. The 635 repeated that pattern, even without the benefit of the official works entries that forced the pace of the original CSL's development into its final winged 3.5 litre form. However the 635 raced in two distinct eras and by 1984 we could see that God had not donated the right to BMW to win distance events without further factory effort. When this was written it remained to be seen if the BMW Motorsport GmbH would ever wake from its Formula I success into defending the company's reputation against revitalised Jaguar, startling turbo Volvos and Roving Rovers.

The first period in BMW 635 CSi's racing history was simply as the current replacement to CSL, which ran out of homologation at the close of 1979. Originally it had been thought that the CSL would cease racing in 1978 and a lot of plans, including Broadspeed's return to European racing after an abortive two seasons racing the Jaguar XJC saloon, were based on the anticipation that the obsolete CSL would be retired. Former Jaguar developer and driver Andy Rouse told me in 1984,' that CSL was such a good *racing* car, it was very hard to make a second a lap on it – which was what we needed for an extra fuel stop on that Jag to win over European distances.'

So the 635 had to follow a top class BMW act in racing, a role BMW had not foreseen for it at the design stage.

I saw the racing Group 2 BMW 635 CSi in European trim for the first time at Brands Hatch in April 1980. By then the car, run by Racing Corporation Vienna, for Umberto Grano, Herbie Werginz and Harald

The nearest thing there was to a factory 6-Series in 1984: the Schnitzer brothers of Freilassing coupé in full flight at Monza's opening round, driven by Hans Stuck and Dieter Quester. The car proved far less competitive in the opening half of the 1984 season versus strong opposition from Jaguar (in their third European season and running three V12 coupés), the 330 horsepower Volvos with water injection and turbocharging, plus the V8 Rovers. The BMW was much as for 1983 with a consistent 285bhp, which simply was not enough. The factory loyalty to Dunlop looked expensive on lap times too. In July 1984 Hans Stuck told reporters, 'we have tested 10 tyres and there is an advantage of 8/10th of a second per lap for the Italian Pirelli tyres.'

BMW coupé of the previous CSL 24-valve type racing versus a similarly powerful Capri RS3100 and Porsche 911 RS in the USA. Such activities spread the BMW name a little further, but also developed the DOHC inline six to a 430bhp pitch, forerunner of today's exciting engine of similar principles in M635 (below).

The most successful European Touring Car Championship driver has been BMW loyalist Dieter Quester, who won his most recent title in a BMW 635 CSi at the age of 44. That was in 1983, when he reckoned to have spent 25 years in motorsport, with two teenage sons (Alexander and Andreas) set to follow Father's trail. Quester won class titles in the European series with the 2002 in 1968, the 2002 turbo in 1969 and outright titles with the CSL coupés (versus Jaguar in 1977) and 1983, with a Schnitzer-prepared Group 635.

144

Neger, had won the opening two rounds (Italy's Monza and Vallelunga qualifiers), but was destined only to win another event that year, leaving a 320i BMW for Helmut Kelleners and Siggi Muller the 1980 European title.

At this stage the car weighed about 1190kg/2618lbs. and had some 367bhp from a factory developed two valve per cylinder engine, Group 2 regulations having outlawed the homologation of special cylinder head options like those of 1974 onward, unless the manufacturer could prove he was making the statutory 1000 cars a year equipped with such power units.

In 1980 this Viennese-based green 635 largely raced on its own in the big class, although there was a 450 SLC Mercedes from time to time. By September 1980 and the annual Tourist Trophy round at Silverstone, the original Austrian 635 had been joined by a car for Belgian Eddy Joosen, both BMWs entered by BMW Italia. They practised faster than anyone else in the 45-car entry, which include some of the modified Rover V8s that were to become the basis of British race winning. The Silverstone round was won by the Grano/Werginz/Neger combo at an average of over 102mph for 3 hours, 4 minutes 12.36 seconds, but it is important to recall that European saloon car races of that period were nothing like so competitive as they have been since Jaguar arrived in 1982.

In 1981 there was some back door Munich support again for the 635 CSi in Group 2. This time the chosen recipients were Switzerland's Eggenberger Motorsport, who prepared an immaculate white coupé for German veteran Helmut Kelleners and Italy's Umberto Grano to run under Enny leather goods sponsorship. They won five of eight European Championship rounds, one with the aid of former World motorcycle Champion Johnny Cecotto. As a model the 635 also won another round and Grano/Kelleners would be European Champions, but the opposition was still not consistently worthy of any stronger interest from BMW. It's worth noting that the 1981 Silverstone Tourist Trophy was won by Tom Walkinshaw/Chuck Nicholson in a Mazda RX7, but Walkinshaw was even then negotiating to overcome Jaguar's lack of finance. Tom interested the Coventry marque in a comeback to the series they first won in 1963 . . . with German drivers!

For 1982 BMW could offer only the 528i for the new group A

regulations. These insisted on production of 5000 cars a year, instead of Group 2's 1000, and featured freedom of modification in suspension (so long as the standard mounting points were retained), braking (ie: you could replace drum brakes with disc), but a more restrained approach to engine modification (amounting to a freedom to modify rather than replace with completely different principles) and few transmission choices. At least, those were the principles...

Grano and Kelleners stuck with BMW and Eggenberger at Guem-lingen in Switzerland whilst BMW Motorsport provided a basic kit of parts—racing suspension with centre lock wheels; high ratio steering

Some of the BMW racers in Dieter Quester's and BMW's ascent of the touring car classes. Car 17 is a 2000 TI four door, a winner at the Spa 24 hours – but for Jackie Ickx/Hubert Hahne – in which Quester had his first works drive. That was in 1966 and he wrote the car off at Nurburgring! Then we have the BMW 2002-registered racer, at Brands Hatch in 1969, where Quester scored a very narrow win in Europe's first regular turbo racer. Finally the immaculate green Gösser Beer Alpina CSL Coupé at Monza is from his 1977 season, which resulted in the outright European title for touring car drivers.

rack; five speed competition Getrag gearbox; replacement braking system with dual master cylinders; differentials with up to 75 per cent locking action from ZF and even a body prepared without primer to accept a roll cage that was useful not only for crash protection, but in preserving general body strength for a four door saloon car asked to withstand 145mph stresses from a 2.8 litres providing no more than 250bhp.

It was an experimental year, a debut season, for the new European racing regulations and BMW found that Jaguar had their lowline XJ-S 5.3 litre V12 in action, being transferred from the earlier Group 1 production saloon car class! Such coupés were assembled by Tom Walkinshaw's TWR concern at Kidlington in England and Walkinshaw had not been the slightest bit retarded in learning from his driving and developing spells with Ford, BMW, Mazda and Austin Rover products. That first season saw the Jaguars win four races and the BMW 528s the rest of the 11 rounds in European countries such as Britain, Belgium, Italy, Austria, Germany – and a trip behind the iron curtain to Czechoslovakia and Brno's fabulous public road track. A circuit second only to the old Nurburgring in driver challenge, and a very fast track that provided Jaguar's first European win for the XJ-S.

By now public interest in group A and European saloon car racing had been rekindled. For years BMW had ruled the roost after defeating Ford in their classic 1973 confrontation. Without serious opposition Munich had naturally kept their factory talents for outlets like European Formula 2, the McLaren-BMW 320-Turbo project in the USA and Europe, and the increased workload that Formula 1 demanded when it was clear that Talbot were not going to be given a ready-made BMW Grand Prix engine (April 1980).

Now it was obvious that an increase in pace over what was possible from 2.8 litres in a substantial four door was needed, if BMW were to maintain their record of providing the Champion European saloon car driver with his motor car in every year bar one (1974: Ford Escort) since 1973.

Since BMW Motorsport had design-manufactured larger engine 5-Series, including the production 535i of 1979-81, it might have been readily assumed that a $3\frac{1}{2}$ litre four door would be forthcoming, the 5-Series itself revamped in 1981. Even in Summer 1984 we were still

148

The duel of 1983: Jaguar's V12 XJ-S coupé of 5.3 litre versus the 3.5 litre BMW 635s. This is the Italian Vallelunga track and the TWR Jaguar is pursued by the BMW Champions of 1982 (in a 528i) Umberto Grano and Helmut Kelleners. By the end of the year BMW had won 6 races and the driver's title; Jaguar had five victories. Yet it was obvious that a 5.3 litre V12 of 400 plus horsepower was not going to be denied by a 3.5 litre six in the long term . . .

waiting for the second generation 535i to materialise . . .

The answer was the 635 CSi. Originally BMW felt there was 'no way' the 6-Series would reach the production level of 5000 a year needed for the German authorities to back an application to FISA in Paris, but the revival of interest in the Sixes since the Summer 1982 facelift allowed BMW to apply for recognition. Yes I *know* the numbers don't add up, but neither did Jaguar's when homologation was granted! That's the way of the racing world and both BMW or Jaguar representatives get extremely heated and prove black is definitely white if questioned on such matters. Besides which, we wouldn't have the splendid *racing* series of today without the Jaguar and BMW coupé prime contenders, both of which can be ruled ineligible on the question of interior space if the rules are applied ruthlessly ... This was very nearly the case prior to the opening of the 1984 European Championship season, and we did lose a number of American coupés as a result, albeit as temporarily as proved to be the case for the oft-threatened Mazda RX7 Group A 'saloon'.

So, ready for 1983 and a Jaguar team that would run two cars all season, rather than their exploratory single entry joined by a second from 1982 Spa 24 Hours (July) onward, BMW put together a Group A racing 635 CSi. As ever they looked back on previous practice and some components in the braking and chassis areas did owe parentage to the legendary Group 2 CSL breed, but basically they had the job of supplying equipment to enable everyone from wealthy amateurs to paid professionals a reliable and competitive long distance racing saloon. Although BMW Motorsport designed components specifically to resist the ravages of long distances in European Championship rounds, the longest being Belgium's annual 24 hour classic at the Spa-Francorchamps circuit, the 6-Series has also been used with success in shorter German and British national title series, and in much-modified form for the premier series of France. Here radical engineering changes can be made and minimum weights play a big part in French competitiveness, or lack of it, in contenders such as Rover and BMW, faced with national specialities like Peugeot's 505 GTI turbo.

Although BMW's sporting engineers knew what they were looking for and drew up the majority of the changes, some work was subcontracted. The most obvious was the task of race-modifying the Group A six cylinder engine, for Formula 1 was absolutely Priority One inside BMW Motorsport and outside help for saloon car racing was needed. Although multiple European Championship winners Alpina at Buchloe – less than an hour's drive west of Munich – were obvious choices, particularly as their superb light green CSL had been Jaguar's downfall in 1977, Alpina boss Burkard Bovensiepen was not terribly tempted by the prospect of running racing cars again. However, he did agree that his burgeoning wine business and the construction of 500 Alpina-BMW road cars a year (including 60 of the fabled 330bhp/160mph plus B7-coded turbo 6-Series) could be joined by a development programme for the A-motor. BMW themselves had run various higher power combinations during development of course, and this information, particularly useful for re-programming the Bosch Motronic's electronic 'brain' and in finding appropriate ignition and injection settings was to provide a starting point for Alpina's work.

Germany's Helmut Kelleners and Italy's Umberto Grano did not have so much luck in their Eggenberger of Switzerland-prepared 635 CSi during 1983, as they had with the same company's 528 the previous season, but this coupé was always a front runner. Here the coupé is conducted by Kelleners at the 1983 Tourist Trophy in Britain, in which it practised sixth quickest and finished in that position, as well.

By Spring 1984 Alpina had delivered over 25 of these six cylinder race units, customers varying from leading European Championship contenders to British BMW loyalists like Frank Sytner at Nottingham. The Sytner brothers are the Alpina agents in Britain for retail customers – besides being one of the largest BMW retailers in the UK. Group A work, with its many restrictions in engineering modifications compared with pure racing engines, or even the saloon car racing units of the sixties and seventies, is not appealing to an organisation of Alpina's capabilities, but the link with BMW is a valued feature of their everyday business life. Thus motors were available from the March 1983 opening Championship round in the European series, held at Monza.

The 3430cc engine was used from the start, but with a maximum tolerance this can measure 3475cc when a bore of 92.6mm, instead of production's 92mm is utilised: the crankshaft throw remains at 86mm. The seven bearing bottom end with its steel construction of crankshaft, twelve counterweights, and steel connecting rods remains, but new pistons from Mahle provide an 11:1 maximum compression.

The big changes in the engine's breathing capacity come from the 324° duration camshaft profile which actuates 46mm inlet and 38mm exhaust valves, in conjunction with reprogrammed Motronic and fuel injection, allowed to pass increased air and fuel flow rates to the carefully ported cylinder head and manifolding. Basically Burkard Bovensiepen's attitude to the black art of working on such restricted engines was his 1984 riposte: 'we have nothing written down about these engines, because with Group A you simply don't write about such things!'

Nicely finished 635 CSi for Frank Sytner was prepared by Ted Grace International and is seen here in its second 1984 season at Thruxton, heading one of the two CC Racing BMW coupés that were fielded by BMW in Britain for Vince Woodman (who missed some rounds) and James Weaver. Only Weaver had won a race for BMW 'on-track' since the Group A ruling started in the UK during 1983, but Sytner's car was always a front runner.

For 1983 the engine generated 285bhp at 6000rpm, a 67bhp bonus over production, and 257lb.ft. of torque, a gain of 29lb.ft. but at 1000rpm higher, were enough to do a stolidly competitive job. In fact the peak horsepower figure was within one of the four valve roadgoing engine in M635. Not bad, but not enough for 1984, and never enough to do more than stay in touch with the Jaguars up to the race car's maximum of just over 150mph. Then the 5.3 litre V12s of the English coupés would sing sweetly off to just over 160mph in the closing stages of each straight piece of track.

Helping in the fight against such a formidable opponent were some of

The ingenious livery for the Genuine BMW Parts (No. 1) Schnitzer coupé of 1983/84 is fully appreciated in this London Art Tech, Steven Tee, study of the car shared to third place in the 1984 Spa Francorchamps 24 hours. Driven by James Weaver/Hans Stuck/Dieter Quester, it had qualified fourth fastest and finished third. Here it passes the eventual 18th placed 635 CSi of an amateur team typical of those who purchased the basic bits to turn a 635 into a Group A racing car. At this event alone there were 17 BMW 635s entered, and 11 finished in the top twenty after 24 hours of very tough racing. Bruno Giacomelli even took fastest lap in another 635, but in 1984 Spa was added to the Jaguar victory total.

the best proven braking and suspension parts in the business, plus an enormous weight bonus. Instead of a production 1430kg/3146lbs. the 635 racer, complete with beautifully crafted aluminium roll cage to pull everything together, weighed in at under 1185kg/2607lbs., the legal minimum for the class. So it had to be ballasted with lead for shorter events. The Jaguar weighed 1400kg/3080lb. at the start of the 1984 season and offered at least 420bhp at the start of the 1984 season. Actually some 420bhp at 6800rpm, with a minimum of 400lb.ft. of torque available from 4400rpm.

BMW specified a Getrag five speed gearbox with the following competition ratios: first, 2.330: second, 1.675; third, 1.353; fourth, 1.146; fifth, 1.00. There was a choice of three final drive ratios including the 3.07 and 3.45 used in 6-Series production and a 3.91 unit for very tight circuits. Complementing a very strong transmission layout was a ZF limited slip differential torqued to 75 per cent.

The suspension owed quite a lot to the 528i saloon of 1982 and some tests were performed taking advantage of the interchangeability between the 5-Series saloon and the coupé, the saloon equipped with 3.4 litre running gear for some initial test work, before the race-prepared 6-Series shell was available.

In Group A the principles of MacPherson front struts and trailing arm rear suspension have to be maintained in a BMW. Completely new hubs designed to take single nut racing wheels, big brakes, and the stresses generated by freshly fabricated suspension arms front and rear, are a must. The big, box-section, rear trailing arms are quite a contrast to the steel stampings of production, as are the spring rates, with the availability of front springs rated beyond 1000lb. inch. At the back, spring rates of around 700lb. could well be employed, with the Bilstein gas-filled damping that was also used for the front strut inserts. Mix in solid mounting bushes for the accurate location, not only of the suspension but also of the rear differential, and the usual racing ball joints where applicable, and you have a Six that feels as though it has been cemented to the track without much in the way of absorption in between the well-equipped cabin (height and distance adjustable race Recaro seats were common) and the 16inch diameter × 11inch wide BBS wheels. Usually shod with Dunlop slicks if you had Munich support, but BMW Italia always went the Pirelli route, with success.

Brakes? A fully bias adjustable (ie front to rear) braking system with cockpit control of anything up to 332mm/13inch fronts and 315mm/12.4inch rears, all of ventilated disc type, could be supplied. There were some slightly smaller discs also optionally specified for racing, supplies coming either from AP in Britain or Ate in Germany. Steering utilised the standard ratio, but power assistance was normally deleted: the only exception I know of in 1983 was Hans Stuck's European mount for some of the longer events, which did have the production derived power assistance, a preference continued in 1984.

So, a lot of modifications, but the end result still looked very much like a Six series and the engine would happily paddle around at race paddock speeds in this comparatively low stage of tune. The reduction in weight helped performance significantly, for the increase in power was not that much by racing standards: *auto motor und sport* tried an early car in 1983, factory supplied, and found the racing first gear and standard clutch plate allowed an acceleration time of only just below 7 seconds from rest to 60mph. European Championship races have a rolling start, so the cars are no dragsters. From rest to 100mph would take just over $13\frac{1}{2}$ seconds and the standing quarter mile, about a second longer.

Fuel consumption? Actually pretty good and the reason why BMW often won in Europe, for they would often save a pit stop or two compared to Jaguar in 1983. The usual BMW range would be from 6.9 to 7.1mpg at a track like Britain's Donington Park.

The 1983-84 record

With the Jaguars in their second season and BMW debuting a new coupé around proven principles there was the recipe for some spicy races in 1983. As ever in saloon car racing there was plenty of off-track battling over legality, but there was no doubt that the crowds started to come back to watch this category, along with increased TV and other media coverage. Jaguar sales in Germany, their target in recent years after the success of sales in America had been realised, really did leap forward. The wholly-owned subsidiary that Jaguar formed for trading in the 1984 German market capitalised on the sales success that this often overlooked category of racing can provide for a motor manufacturer.

The last Nurburgring 6 Hours to be held on the old 14 mile track was the 1983 event, which saw BMW 635s finish in the first six places! This is the third fastest car in practice (7m 58.27 secs) of German ATS Formula 1 driver Manfred Winkelhock and Austrian Dieter Quester. They won by a lap, at an average over 93mph.

March 20th 1983 and, ten years after BMW began their successful season of mastery over Ford, a new era opened with Jaguar as the opponent for BMW coupés. The 500km/310.5 mile Monza opener displayed the strength of BMW's appeal to racing customers with eight 635s in the top ten finishers, including the winning coupé of Dieter Quester/Carlo Rossi. Yet Jaguar's twins returned with a second place for Tom Walkinshaw/Chuck Nicholson, just 4.7 seconds adrift . . . and Tom Walkinshaw grasped the fastest lap.

The contestants seemed at their most balanced that 1983 season. BMW won five races, prior to the Belgian final round at Zolder on September 25th, and so had Jaguar! I was lucky enough to go to that final, actually with the Rover 3500 V8 team who had been the only others to score a Championship round win that season. The spectacle of so many 'tin-tops' weaving their way around the 2.648 mile track, that's also used for Grand Prix, was right in the rivetting category.

Some 16 front runners–including the two Jaguars, a pair of Rovers, a single Mustang and some of the astounding turbo Volvos amongst the BMW 635 majority–practised within the same 2.5second band, but with a 46 car field there were plenty of other dices throughout the field to keep a wary eye on whilst also trying to photograph for *Motoring News*. A man could die taking BMW v Jag pix whilst a Belgian tin box slithered across the grass with some more playmates, intent on taking you out, should the first man miss! The Belgians put me on the deck the following year . . . !

Hans Stuck in the tattered Cheylesmore 635 after a fraught battle to the finish of 1983 Brands Hatch British Championship round, a race that went on the day to Steve Soper's Rover V8. It took until 1984 to legally clarify the results of the British series (!) after a protracted series of off-track battles between the RACSMA, Ted Grace International (preparers of Frank Sytner's racing 635) and Tom Walkinshaw Racing. TWR were also the company who prepared the V12 Jaguars, as well as the 1983/84 Rover V8s. In 1984 penalties of £100,000 were imposed on TWR and the fuel injection Vitesse models were disqualified retrospectively from all British events they entered after May 29th 1983, to the close of the season. The majority of qualifying rounds, in other words.

Bound to end in tears. . . . James Weaver, in 635 number 14 from Hartge Motorsport at Aachen, takes on Peter Lovett's TWR Rover into the Woodcote chicane at Silverstone. The Rover finished up in the wall at this 1983 Tourist Trophy whilst the BMW, shared by Formula 2 Champion Jonathan Palmer, finished second.

BMW had 1984 Tyrell Grand Prix ace Stefan Bellof as their secret weapon in a one-off appearance in a new Schnitzer of Freilassing prepared CSi. After an initial sprint from the Jaguars and the rival BMW for Helmut Kelleners/Umberto Grano, Bellof took over and led until his retirement after only 35 laps. However, there were plenty more 635s where that one came from, and the British contingent, Rover or Jaguar, had swiftly succumbed to the lure of the dreary pits . . .

The closing laps were fantastically exciting, owing to Belgium's great organisational talents providing us with a race run in twilight around the wreckage of various immobile hulks. We and many of the lap scorers felt that Win Percy in the Jaguar was closing in during the final laps, despite gearbox malfunctions, but the on-paper result showed an all-BMW squad from first to seventh, the Jag only eighth.

Dieter Quester won the title *again*, performing the equivalent of a ground loop in his Schnitzer car as it weaved past the pits and the chequered flag. BMW had provided the winning car for 14 drivers in 18 European Touring Car Championship seasons! You have to make a tough and consistently quick car to put in a record like that, whatever the standard of opposition . . .

In Britain the 635 CSi did not have an easy introduction to British Group A, for that man Walkinshaw had a team of solidly entrenched Rover V8s, that became fuel-injected for 1983 in Vitesse guise. The result was a season in which Austin Rover apparently won every round, but the legal wrangling went completely 'over the top' and the outright Champion had still to be declared, seven *months* after the final race was run! The main controversy was over the legality of the Rovers and involved a pitched battle between Austin Rover and TWR versus Frank Sytner's BMW team and the British organising authority, a division of the Royal Automobile Club. Austin Rover finally renounced all claim to

This is what that British Championship battle looked like at Donington in 1983: Stuck leads Soper's Rover, with Win Percy's Toyota Supra and Frank Sytner's BMW also topping 140mph on the run down to the chicane.

Schnitzer also prepared this Wurth-backed BMW 635 for European Championship racing to the usual factory recommended specification for Group A. Even Manfred Winkelhock couldn't make it a winner in the first half of 1984 . . .

the 1983 titles in June 1984 . . . and TWR were fined £10,000- plus £90,000 in costs.

For BMW the 1983 British season involved former BMW CSL-Alpina entrant Malcolm Gartlan, who managed a car built by Ted Grace for Frank Sytner, a combination that continued in 1984. In 1983 there was also a Cheylesmore/BS fabrications 635 CSi to factory specification that was run for Hans Stuck on a number of occasions and that twice nearly beat the all-conquering combination of Steven Soper plus Rover.

However the honour of scoring the first non-Rover win since the advent of Group A in Britain for 1983 had to wait until 1984. On Spring Bank Holiday's Good Friday, Formula 3 hotshoe James Weaver took the BMW GB/CC Racing 635 CSi to a flag-to-flag victory around the tricky Oulton Park Circuit. As this was written the works Rovers had been withdrawn, but Andy Rouse in the ICS-sponsored example was still winning privately.

160

In Europe 1984 was a disaster for the 635 CSi during the opening months, for enough power was simply not legally obtainable to stay in touch with the turbocharged Volvo, fleet but fragile Rovers, and the pace-setting Jaguars. The TWR team had now reaped the reward of racing much the same car since 1982. The scoreline when this was written read a dismal 4-1 in favour of Jaguar. Just how bad things were at the end of June could be seen at the Austrian Oesterreichring, in which qualifying saw not a single BMW in the top ten! Even at the end there was only a third place reward behind two Jaguars, but even that had sometimes been denied in the opening races of 1984 because Jaguar were running three of the green and white XJS V12s . . .

Something had to be done, but The Answer from BMW was not known when this was written. For BMW Motorsport were busy pulling themselves back into the real world, after Nelson Piquet had ended a long lean 1984 spell in Grand Prix Racing via two American wins.

Technically the specialists like Schnitzer, Alpina and Hartge could provide the extra power that the 635 is particularly capable of reliably absorbing, but whether BMW had the willpower to gain international recognition for new engine parts was a different matter.

For the 6-Series itself was nearing the end of its production span by this stage, and the future in saloon car racing looked to lie with lightweight cars of the Mercedes 2.3/16-Cosworth type, or with a turbo. BMW were rumoured to have an answer to the Mercedes compact powerhouse ready for production in 1985 and possible for racing use . . . but not until 1986. Another 20bhp would lift the 635's pace toward that of its 1984 rivals, but it was not certain if BMW Motorsport would sanction such moves, because that would inevitably require new paperwork and parts.

As a European winner in 1980/81 and 1983, the BMW coupé earned its sporting spurs the hard way, but the going gets tougher all the time in international motorsport . . .

Chapter Eight

'Freude am Fahren'

The phrase is a well-used BMW advertising and publicity brochure tag line that literally means Joy through Driving, and the 6-Series miles and kilometres I have been allowed have certainly lived up to that expectation.

The least powerful model I have driven regularly was the 633 CSi in its original four speed gearbox RHD trim, whilst the most horsepower belonged to a B7 Alpina turbo borrowed in 1982 and driven back-to-back with the then new 3.4 litre 635. The former had some 197bhp and was capable of about 135mph with quite a lot of unspoilered weaving going on in motorway crosswinds and under heavy braking, owing to that original front suspension arrangement. Because I was going to miss a plane, for the first and so far last time, the 633 CSi was driven harder than I have ever driven before, or since. Not faster, because the M635 regularly romped up to 150mph plus, even on a short trip out to Munich airport, or gallivanting to Garmisch, but harder because everything the manufacturer provided was fully utilised all the dawn motoring time in that 633 CSi.

Then the 633 was just under £15,000 in Britain and there were plenty of critics who said, much as Americans first commented of the 630 CSi, it didn't have enough of anything to rate a price in the Mercedes class. From a driver's viewpoint there was the familiar BMW or Mercedes feeling of getting into the newcomer and wondering for the first few miles where all the money had been absorbed? Compared with British ideas of luxury there is a dearth of plush items such as wood cappings and a great deal of neatly-installed plastic instead. Also, you can really hear the engine, versus the Jeeves-like sibilant tones of a Jaguar, and then there are seats made to support over hundreds of hard autobahn

Behind the wheel of Hans Stuck's 1983 Group A racing 635 CSi the cockpit layout is a little different and the noise levels toward rude! This beautifully prepared example of the 635 racer typifies the attractions many BMW Motorsport customers find in a logically laid out basis for racing that has proved itself particularly in the longer European Championship rounds. Approximately 50 racing 635s to Group A specification have been sold from Munich.

miles, rather than showroom seduction. In the case of the 6-Series the fascia layout attracted a good deal of initial attention and praise. The test system of 1976, with its pushbutton input, could be regarded as the nearest BMW have got to gimmicks, but the matchless central speedometer (electronic and a model of accuracy versus most rivals) and flanking dials for rpm and the combined water temperature/fuel gauge, have still to be bettered in my opinion. On present form it does not look as though digital electronics are going to provide a cleaner and more legible system either.

As in today's cars the lasting impressions were of a good manual gearchange. Or the usefulness of a dashboard indicator of automatic gearbox selection (now, sadly, deleted) and an excellent driving position, with a slight amelioration of the BMW 'on top-of-the-situation, Kommandant' stance in favour of lowline coupé posture.

163

I cannot say the original 633 ever felt slow to me, an eight second 0–60mph level of acceleration then unlikely in the hot hatchback class: the RHD Golf GTI did not arrive in the UK until July 1979! However the sometimes hoarse engine and the ease with which the chassis could be moved by crosswinds and determined use of brakes or low gear throttle, did not strike me as progress. Or competitive with machinery such as the Jaguar XJS, and it was disturbing to hear about the quality problems at Karmann, because my then-employers at *Motor Sport* purchased an early RHD CSi, which had been specially imported. BMW in Britain were spared any embarrassment on this score, for the car was sold more swiftly than seemed decent at the time, for reasons that had nothing to do with the car's quality.

The original 3.5 litre 635 arrived with me in 1979, by which time it was closer to £19,000. However, the firmer suspension and extra spoilers wrought such a feeling of extra security that every penny seemed worthwhile. The bright red coupé spent some time gambolling on British roads, between snow storms, with impressive acceleration and

My first encounter with the 6-Series was this 1976 demonstrator, seen here propping up the spelling editor.

LHD and RHD cockpit contrast belong to the Munich-registered M635 with its unique Motorsport three spoke steering wheel, and the automatic 635 CSi used to and from Munich. Contrast in driving one after the other is immense, the M-coupé surprisingly having a better ride coupled to that superior suspension, but M635 is undeniably hard traffic work compared with svelte automatic. The harder you drive, the better the M635 becomes . . .

*Thrills galore! Alpina's turbocharged 3430cc now gives 330bhp, 0–62mph in 5.9 secs,
164mph and adjustable boost for the man who likes to help Alpina owner Burkard
Bovensiepen chuckle a little more on the way to his favourite Buchloe bank.*

100 per cent confirmation of its 140mph capabilities. The five speed
gearbox actually allowed an improvement to be noted over the less
powerful four speed 633 in terms of fuel consumption, so the whole
exercise was worthwhile.

The next 635 I drove was the revised 3.4 litre engine, featuring a five
speed wide ratio gearbox and LHD. We spent a morning in the Munich
suburbs and then took advantage of the now extraordinary refinement
and much improved economy to dash down to Buchloe. At short notice
we borrowed Herr Bovensiepen's B7 coupé, then with 3 litres
developing 300bhp, spending the rest of the day swopping cars with my
UK colleague Peter Newton.

Driving the Alpina car was hard work compared to the production
CSi, but certainly exhilarating. The combination of a five speed sports
Getrag gearbox and a tall 2.93 final drive ratio in the back axle allowed
47mph in first gear, 78mph in second, 112mph in third, and 140mph in

a fourth gear at the 6500rpm limit . . . And then you shifted into fifth and felt this sombrely-sprayed 'Mean machine' track toward an indicated 250km/h . . . Some 155mph!

The car certainly looked the part on 16inch diameter alloy wheels with seven and eight inch wide rims, 205/55 front tyres or even lower profile 225/50 Pirellis at the back. There were appropriate suspension modifications built around Bilstein dampers, but today's B7 coupé is quicker still. Now they have the 3430cc six cylinder engine as the basic unit, with intercooling and KKK turbocharging now part of the reprogrammed Bosch Motronic's provence.

The result in 1984 is 330bhp at 5800rpm, a 5.9seconds claim for the 0-62mph acceleration time and a maximum speed of 165.8mph. Each of these individually labelled Alpina BMW B7 coupés cost the equivalent of £31,099 in Germany in May 1984 and demand seemed totally unaffected by BMW's own super coupé, M635. I haven't experienced the latest 330hp mechanical specification in the coupé, but I did drive

Half the art in Group A racing, or in extracting further power from the production engine by turbocharging, is to get the computer to understand the engine's new needs. Here is the Alpina version of Motronic management.

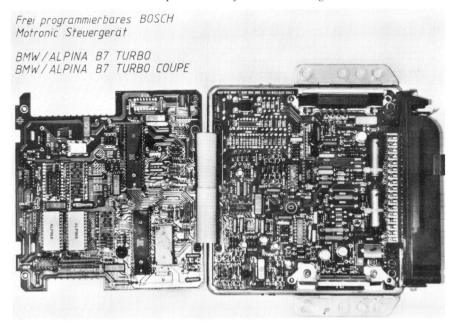

*The B9 conversion features a conventionally modified 3.4 litre Alpina rendering of the
BMW six that is instantly rewarding and easier for the stranger to drive fast,
immediately, than the turbo. The engine gives 245bhp at 5700rpm, enough to nudge
150mph and leap from rest to 60mph in some 6½ seconds, and was priced individually
at £2578 on the Summer 1984 exchange rate.*

the similar 3.4 litre B7 Turbo installation with the large KKK-K27
turbo and its attendant intercooling in an Alpina 5-Series (actually I
drove two such cars, one being an automatic). My shaky handwriting
says that it was 'impressive to 3100rpm, whence it is capable of
destroying the civilised world, as we know it . . ' When that thing gets
on boost, even Pirelli's biggest rubber boots whimper and you need
hands that can twirl a steering wheel every which way but the Police
Academy driving way . . .

Next came the research for this book and a packed six day trip to
Germany from the UK. Plus a few more days running around at home in
the four speed ZF automatic-equipped 635 CSi that represented a basic
£25,000 without extras, although to be fair the only significant option on
that list for most customers would have been to add air conditioning.

I clocked up 1643 miles in that coupé and the tank-filling average
worked out at 23.13mpg. I used the standard onboard computer for only
12 hours of journey time at an average 67mph, and that displayed
23.5mpg. Figures that I find very impressive for a car that was rarely

The B7 Turbo from Alpina can be boosted from 250 to 330bhp by turning the cockpit handwheel. Unfortunately Herr Bovensiepen has neglected to equip my cheque book with the same instant resourcefulness. For the man who has everything and wants to get away from it, fast.

cruised below 100mph on the continent, and that spent something like two hours tearing toward Munich with a Porsche 944, as close to 140mph continuous pace as the cars could reach.

The automatic gearbox is superbly mated with that excellent and widely spread pulling power. If you shift into the S for Sport mode, acceleration is exactly as for the Porsche 944 between 60mph and 130mph, whilst the normal wider spacing of the economy-orientated E-setting provides effortless town and country shift of a superior quality that ZF users from the seventies would never recognise.

The TRX tyres and alloy wheels were not so well-mated to a suspension that proved harsher and jerkier in ride quality than that of M635, but it did provide excellent motorway handling through the kind of long fast bends that you can only legally tackle at BMW speeds in its native land. Only once did I find too much tail-happiness for public road comfort, and that was when I trod on the accelerator briskly on a dry but cramped roundabout. The big BMW swatted about vigorously at the

169

Scene of many 635 motor racing victories in the annual 24 hour race at Spa-Francorchamps, the BMW stops on the public road that leads to the circuit.

Seaborne 635 takes the Townsend Thorensen Dover-Ostend voyage of over 4 hours, back to Germany, where Real Cars Eat Motorways *before breakfast.*

'Freude am Fahren'

Coupés are all about images, and this one of the 635 CSi is the kind of pleasant memory that lingers on after the dream machine has returned to headquarters.

Averaging close to 100mph on the clearer sections of South German autobahnen, *the 635 pauses for thought and fuel during its daylight ground flight to Munich.*

Details on loan M635 CSi show that they changed from simply putting BMW on the engine rocker cover twice to MPower legend. From here the well protected distributor, feeding six plugs, is in the foreground and the exhaust's serpentine sweeps are obviously vital to fit beneath that traditional slanted cylinder block. Wheels are the 8.3in. × 13.98in. light alloy BBS rims with cast centres and 240/45 VR Michelin TRX rubber. Wet or dry, they do an impressive job.

back, but the usual speed-sensitive power steering contained its wrath neatly and enjoyably.

Finally, my personal favourites both had some 285 horsepower, give or take a pony. The M635 was just as demanding as Alpina's turbo had been, and it didn't look as though we were going to get along at first. Our opening mileage was to plod to Dingolfing and back in the rain, a journey up from Munich that contains a lot of lorry-infested two-way roads.

Under such circumstances it pays to be extremely precise with the clutch and throttle during gearchanges on the racing pattern Getrag, especially when shifting from first to second gears across the gate, where it's all too easy to jerk passenger's necks around as the rpm drop very suddenly when the heavy action clutch engages with all the finality of a steam hammer. Peter Newton summed up its progress aptly in the pages of *Cars & Car Conversions* when he said, 'quite simply it has enormous low speed torque, peaking with 251lb.ft. at 4500rpm, so it just picks itself up like a giant stirring from winter slumber and hurls this very substantial chunk of motor car at the horizon like Jeff Capes putting the shot. The figures suggest nothing of this engine's awe-inspiring music: 0-60mph in comfortably under seven seconds; 0-100mph in under 18

We stayed out most of the night, just to drive the M-car a little further . . .

It came from the heart of Bavaria to take the 6-Series another giant step forward: M635 rests on the widest wheel/tyre option.

seconds at which point you change into fourth gear! The latter runs out at 130mph and fifth takes you out on the wild side . . .'

Outstanding memories of two days and a night with the Motorsport masterpiece, include a tremendously capable ride, that shows sport and discomfort do *not* need to be bedfellows (remember the softly sprung Chapman Lotus approach?) and a stability at speed that contrasts with the still gently weaving 100mph plus progress of the usual 635 in a strong motorway crosswind. The brakes were also superb and the general comment of the M635 was that the harder you drove it, the more alive and responsive it became. The engine is perfectly willing to idle at 700rpm, rocking the car like a giant BDA Escort rally car that has been to a charm and deportment school. Yet there is little pleasure in lugging around town with the heavy, truck-like clutch and a gearchange that prefers firm, fast changes. Plus an engine that seems to catch fire at 4000rpm and inspires the driver into all kinds of anti-social habits, just for the hell of repeating that magnificent six cylinder, 24 valve battle cry. If anything the motor sounds louder and harder than it did in the mid-engine M1, presumably because it is in front of you and surrounded by steel panels.

Finally there was the Cheylesmore Motorsport group A635 to savour in August 1983. With Hans Stuck on hand to make sure the car was set up for its weekend appointment with the Rovers at Britain's Donington Park circuit, a picturesque under three mile track that literally runs uphill and down dale, and a perfect day of sunshine, this had to be the best thing since I was allowed some mileage in the earlier racing coupés during the seventies.

Immediately there is that feeling of being at home. The dashboard was covered in dials, but the large VDO tachometer with 7200rpm as a maximum meant most to the stranger tugging at the unassisted steering through a chunky three spoke steering wheel. That the seat would cope instantly with the change from 6ft 2inches and more of Stuck to under 5ft 9inch of me, said how much messrs BMW and Recaro understood about the partnership sizing problems of quick pit stops in long distance races.

Installed in the lefthand seat, the racing gear pattern with first isolated closest to the driver makes more sense than with RHD. The immediate 'in touch' feel given by those vast brakes and rigid suspension meant I

From this angle, the extra wheel arch flare is most obvious.

Bob Sparshott's preparation company allowed this Summer encounter with the 635 CSi Hans Stuck drove to such memorable effect against Steven Soper's Rover in British Championship races of 1983. In 1984 the car appeared in Grundig colours for David Kennedy to contest most UK Championship rounds, but BMWs in Britain have never had the consistent success recorded on the continent.

was able to use 7200 as a regular change point quite quickly, and enjoy the occasional power slide, without coming to any harm, although the brakes on this particular coupé had a very sloppy pedal indeed.

I summed up after 140mph thrills and some best laps in the region of an 81mph average for *Motoring News*: 'the 635? Beautifully finished, it felt the type of long distance hard runner that its record so obviously suggests. BMW has been winning European races for a very long time now. You can feel that total long distance experience through the comfortable driving position and an engine tuned for useable torque, rather than outright horsepower. There's nothing remotely 'flash' about the 635, it works along proven lines, and it works for a large number of customers with an amazing consistency.'

You could say much the same of the racer's elegantly refined road cousins . . .

Parting is such sweet sorrow[2]!